COLLINS COUNTRYSIDE SERIES
ROCKS

These books are intended to offer the beginner a modern introduction to British natural history. Written by experienced field workers who are also successful teachers, they assume no previous training and are carefully illustrated. It is hoped that they will help to spread understanding and love of our wild plant and animal life, and the desire to conserve it for the future.

COLLINS COUNTRYSIDE SERIES

ROCKS

*

David Dineley

COLLINS
ST JAMES'S PLACE, LONDON

William Collins Sons & Co Ltd
London · Glasgow · Sydney · Auckland
Toronto · Johannesburg

TO DR M. E. TOMLINSON

First published 1976
© D. L. Dineley

ISBN 0 00 219354 X

Made and Printed in Great Britain by
William Collins Sons & Co Ltd Glasgow

CONTENTS

PHOTOGRAPHS

PREFACE

In every countryside there is some geology. Crags, cliffs and quarries all bring it to our attention with some force, but even in a landscape where no rock is in sight, geology has been and still is exerting its influence. Our land is carved by water, ice and wind from the solid rock, the clay and sands that have taken an immense time to reach their present state and places. This book is concerned with the minerals, rocks and fossils that lie beneath our feet. They provide the clues to much of the story of how Britain acquired its infinitely variable scenery.

Modern geology began in Britain. A Scot set out 200 years or so ago the basic ideas that still govern much of our thinking about geology and a West Countryman soon afterwards recognized the value of fossils in identifying rock formations in different parts of the country. They both began by simply using their eyes and collecting specimens. We can do the same, and if this slim volume helps to convey the wonderful variety of beautiful things that lie within the ground it will succeed.

D.L.D.

ACKNOWLEDGEMENTS

I owe much to the patience and knowledge of my colleagues at the University of Bristol, who have been kind enough to improve portions of the text and to offer many helpful suggestions. Dr R. Bradshaw has been especially forebearing. To Mrs Alma Gregory I am delighted to offer thanks for her excellent illustrations and to Mrs J. D. Rowland thanks for rendering the manuscript into readable form. Robin Godwin helped with the photographs.

CHAPTER I

INTRODUCTION

ONE of the rather puzzling things said about the exploration of space, the moon and the other planets in recent years is that it will help us better to understand the nature and origin of our own earth. Naturally we are most interested in our home planet, especially since the scientists emphasize that it is unique, unlike any other member of our solar system. No other planet has quite the range of temperatures that earth has, is populated with living things as we know them or can have had a history like the earth's. Although the planets vary in size and composition and travel at different speeds on different orbits, they all seem to belong to a single system. Many of the same chemical elements are present in each and perhaps they have combined to form the same kinds of minerals as there are on earth. But life as we know it seems to be restricted to our own planet, and it is one of the means by which the earth has come to be so different from its solar sisters.

Several thousand million years ago the solar system came into being. It is possible that all the planets were formed at about the same time, but they have differed in their subsequent histories. Earth has been subject to the same laws of physics as the others, influenced by its

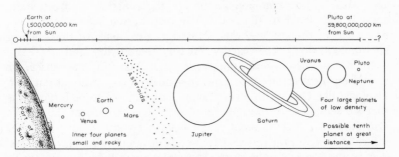

The solar system consists of widely spaced planets revolving round the sun. All have parts that are metallic, parts made of rock and gaseous envelopes. Earth alone seems to have an abundance of water and a vigorous cover of living things. All are shown on the same scale here and their distances from the sun are indicated above. Earth is 12,756 km in diameter.

11

size and distance from the sun, by its moon and perhaps by events taking place elsewhere in space. It has ended up wet and fermenting.

Although the earth may have initially been cold, it passed through a phase early in its history when it was hot and perhaps molten. Water appeared on earth once the temperature dropped below boiling point, and that was probably a long time after the planet first took shape. The fermentation started when the first organic substances were formed and the process began of building increasingly complex molecules into ultimately living matter. Biologists, accepting evolution, acknowledge the unceasing process of change in the living world from the appearance of the first organisms to the present. Geologists see the earth as a continually changing planet, subjected to influences from outside, to changes wrought by the energy concealed within and to the demands and effects of living matter on its surface. We are able to read something of the record and interaction of these different influences in our study of minerals (see page 21), rocks and fossils.

The **minerals** important to technology and man's (or woman's) vanity form, in fact, but a small part of the mineral kingdom. Many of the others are infinitely more abundant or tell us much more about the history of the earth and the nature of matter itself. An important few radioactive minerals by their energy provide the earth with its immense internal forces and also give us an atomic clock by which to measure the millions of years of earth history. **Rocks** are aggregates of minerals in one form or another, and most of earth's record is read from a study of rock composition, origin and destruction.

Fossils, the preserved remains of once living things or their activities, reveal the evolution of life and help us reconstruct the scenes of long ago. Most of the common fossils are the remains of invertebrate animals that lived in the sea. Their distribution tells which rocks originated in the sea, and their character is evidence of the kinds of environment that once existed where now there is dry land.

In an age when exciting things are being found in outer space, we should not neglect the discoveries continually being made at our feet. Geology, like charity, begins at home. One fact not to be forgotten is that we sample only the uppermost five miles (8 km) of the earth's crust, and the planet is about 7926 miles (12,756 km) in diameter! For information about the rest we have to rely on geophysics. Nevertheless, it is in the top few miles of the crust that earth history seems to be written, where rock and water, atmosphere and solar energy have interacted.

GEOLOGICAL TIME

We should give some thought to the time needed for the various events that have brought earth to its present state. Some events, such as a volcanic explosion, happen rapidly; others must have needed tremendous periods of time. 'The Father of Modern Geology', the Scot, James Hutton, living two hundred years ago, suggested that we can interpret the rocks around us in the light of what we see going on today. Assuming that geological changes have fundamentally been the same throughout earth's history and have always gone on at about the rate we see now, we can use the present as the key to the past. It was at once apparent that if Hutton's suggestion is to have any value we need to think in terms of millions of years. All subsequent investigations have confirmed this. In his concept of an ever-changing, evolving world of living things, Charles Darwin also saw that immense spans of time were called for. Despite the objections of the nineteenth-century biblical scholars, science went on to show that a long time has been available. In the twentieth century not only has it become accepted that the earth is many million years old, but means of measuring such periods in years, give or take a few million, has come from the investigation of radioactive minerals. We shall look at this later (pages 71–2).

Meanwhile, to get things into the right order of magnitude, let us stress that, unless the laws governing the behaviour of matter have changed (which is unlikely!), the earth must be around 4500 million years old. We cannot see a way of measuring time before that date, and what happened earlier is not geology. At least that is our excuse for now. The oldest fossils come from rocks 2000–3000 million years old, and the first recognizable fossil animals in any abundance occur in strata around six hundred million years in age; with little more than one million years to his credit, man is a newcomer. These fossils record biological events which took place only when conditions allowed. Before living things could exist, temperatures on earth had to be much as now and water had to be present. Animals could not evolve before plants had developed to provide them with food. The whole evolution of life has to be seen against a background of geological events and conditions. The rocks and minerals set the scene, life plays out its role, fossils result. Life could become extinct one day and only the fossils would then remain – we may be among them.

Of course geological events were taking place long before life appeared. Earth's early history was surely turbulent and perhaps incredibly hot. There may have been almost universal and perpetual

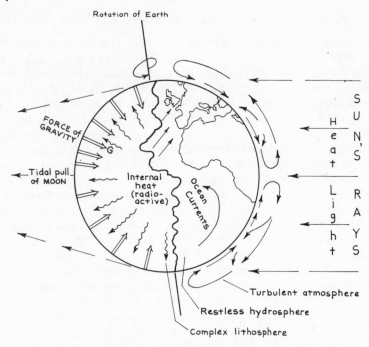

Rotation of Earth

FORCE of GRAVITY

Tidal pull of MOON

Internal heat (radio-active)

Ocean Currents

S U N ' S   R A Y S

Heat

Light

Turbulent atmosphere

Restless hydrosphere

Complex lithosphere

The suffering earth. As it spins on its axis and revolves about the sun the earth is warmed by the sun's rays. The atmosphere and the oceans convect and move in response to this. The moon, circling the earth, pulls the tides to and fro; the movement never ceases. From within the earth gravity exerts its eternal pull while terrestrial heat may melt the crust and set up convection currents in the earth's mantle. The result of these movements is that the crust of the earth is constantly changing.

volcanic eruptions. When these terrestrial tantrums died down, the temperatures dropped sufficiently to allow steam and water vapour from the volcanoes to condense and fall as hot rain on the crust. The sizzling surface became flooded so that the earth would experience all the water-powered processes of rock weathering, erosion and deposition that are so important. In the seas that were to form and cover 70% or more of the earth's surface, new minerals, rocks and ultimately life itself was to be born.

The vestiges of earth's beginnings are all too few and difficult to interpret, but each year we seem to get a little nearer to solving some

		millions of years		GEOLOGICAL PERIODS
PHANEROZOIC EON	CAINOZOIC ERA	− 2 m.y.	The Age of Man	Holocene
				Pleistocene
			The Age of Mammals	Pliocene
				Miocene
				Oligocene
		− 65 m.y.		Eocene
	MESOZOIC ERA		The Age of Reptiles	Cretaceous
				Jurassic
		− 225 m.y.		Triassic
	PALAEOZOIC ERA			Permian
				Carboniferous
			The first amphibia	Devonian
			The first land plants	Silurian
			The first vertebrates	Ordovician
		− 570 m.y.	The first shellfish	Cambrian
CRYPTOZOIC EON	"Precambrian Eras"		The first soft bodied animals	Precambrian
		− 1000 m.y.	The first green algae	
		− 2000 m.y.	The first algal reefs	
		− 3000	The oldest rocks in Britain	
		− 3200	The oldest fossils, blue green algae	
			The oldest unaltered sedimentary rock	
		− 3800	The oldest rocks in the world	
		− 4500 m.y.	Birth of the Earth	

The geological time scale. More than three quarters of the time the earth has existed had passed before life began to leave much trace of its existence upon the planet. The earlier periods saw volcanic upheavals and earth movements on an almost unimaginable scale.

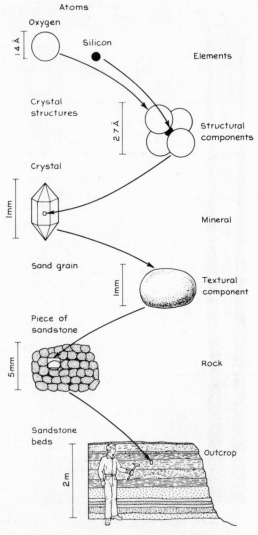

The order of components in a rock. Atoms combine in structural components forming minerals, which in turn are the constituents of rocks. Å = 1 Angstrom unit or 10^{-8} cm, ·00000001 cm. (After Press and Siever).

of the problems. What is certain is that for a very long time this planet was quite unlike the world of today.

Looking forward in time we wonder what may happen to planet earth and, perhaps, what control over its destiny man may have. Our sun is merely a small star among the countless thousands of stars in the galaxy. What happens to earth clearly depends on the fate of the sun. We know that stars evolve, change with time, expand, erupt, wither and diminish into cold deadness. This will happen to the sun. As stars go, it is rather a puny youngster and it still has by all accounts a life of many thousand million years. If its energy were to grow by even a fraction, earth would shrivel and bake; should it fade, a perpetual deep freeze would engulf the globe. Either way means the end of all recognizable life.

MATTER

So much for time. Now we should deal with more tangible matter and see what underlies its behaviour.

Almost every branch of science is concerned with the study of matter. The physicist may claim that his is the study of matter in its most elemental forms – that the other sciences have to take second place. There is something in this because we need some understanding of the nature of matter in order to appreciate its various forms and behaviour. To the geologist considering the character and composition of minerals, the passage of earthquake shocks through the centre of the earth or the transformation of organic matter into petroleum, the need to understand the properties of matter is soon apparent. And indeed a feed-back to physics from the earth-sciences has become important because of the readiness with which geologists have in their own field put concepts of physics to the test. Since we shall be looking at the behaviour of the matter that makes up the earth, it may be worth outlining the nature of the stuff from which everything has somehow been fashioned.

The idea that matter ultimately consists of atoms – the smallest divisible particles of the elements – is of course now quite old. But during the last few decades some of our ideas about the structure of atoms themselves have been undergoing changes. The atom is by no means the solid lump that it was once pictured to be. It is regarded rather as an infinitely small solar system with a central *nucleus* surrounded by numbers of tiny planets known as *electrons*. The electrons move at high speed round the nucleus along *orbitals* which are really

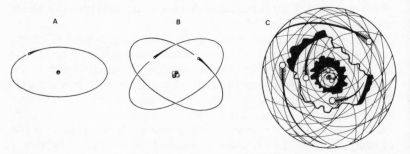

The atomic ball game. Around the dense nucleus of protons and neutrons rush the electrons. Hydrogen (*left*) has a single electron ever chasing around a nucleus of one proton and one neutron: helium (*centre*) has two electrons around a nucleus of two protons and two neutrons. Carbon (*right*) has its six electrons in three shells. In more complex atoms there are more electron shells and the diameter of the shells may be 20,000 to 200,000 times the diameter of the nucleus. The nucleus may be thought of as the sun of the solar system – the electrons, the planets, embrace more space than the rest of the entire solar system.

rather like concentric shells. If you can imagine that the diameter of the electron shell about a nucleus is 10^{-8} cm, it is not much harder to consider the nucleus itself at 10^{-13} cm! The shell is 100,000 times the diameter of the nucleus. In short, most of the atom is space.

Even the nucleus is not a simple entity but contains two principal components. The *protons* each have a single positive charge of energy, while the *neutrons,* as their name suggests, have no charge at all. Different elements have different numbers of protons and neutrons in the nucleus, and in some cases individual atoms of an element have a different number of protons from other atoms of the same element. These individuals are called *isotopes* and they may behave very differently from the 'regular' elements.

While the nucleus has a positive charge (from the protons), the electron cloud whirling around it has a corresponding negative charge. There is a negative electron to match each proton, so the atom as a whole is neutral. Each shell of electrons has a definite capacity for them. The innermost has a capacity of two, the second eight, the third eighteen, and so on. It seems that the amount of energy in each of the electron shells is related to its position relative to the nucleus and that the amount differs from shell to shell. In a *dormant* or *static* atom the electrons all occupy shells of low energy value. In *excited* atoms they may move into outer shells of high energy value, and as they move back into inner shells so energy is given off. Should an atom somehow acquire other electrons from nearby space or lose electrons to space, that atom becomes unbalanced and assumes a positive or a negative charge. In this state we call it an *ion*. Some elements easily lose electrons, while others capture them. Sodium (Na) atoms readily cast off electrons and acquire a positive charge, while chlorine (Cl) atoms grab electrons and receive a negative charge: so Na+ and Cl−. The attractions these atoms have for each other are too great to be resisted and the result is NaCl; the charges cancel out and sodium chloride, salt, is formed.

This is one of the ways in which atoms of different elements link up. It is called *bonding* and the kind of bonding to which elements are prone influences their character. Weak bonds produce soft substances or those that decompose easily. Strong bonds have the opposite effect. In complex molecules involving strongly bonding and weakly bonding elements, as in many minerals, it is the weaker bonds that most influence the mineral's properties. In nature 92 different kinds of atoms exist − providing us with the different elements. Some are rare, others common. Most of these combine within the earth to give the various compounds, and these compounds are known as minerals.

GASES, LIQUIDS AND SOLIDS

These are the states of matter and we need not emphasize how differently the same substance (water, for example) behaves from state to state.

Gases have neither shape nor fixed volume and they normally have a low density and weight. Were it not for earth's gravity they would soon drift off into outer space and we would be left without an atmosphere. Gases can be enormously compressed, and when they are they may be transformed to the liquid state. Gases exert pressure and if a gas is heated the pressure rises, but decreasing the temperature may convert it to a liquid. Finally, gases can diffuse one through another and also through some liquids and solids.

Versatile things, gases! They have played a major role in the evolution of the planet and of life.

Liquids have definite volume but not shape, and will flow into the spaces available to them, although not all liquids flow equally readily. The density of liquids is much greater than that of gases and they are almost incompressible. On the other hand, they do evaporate – turn into gases – when the temperature or pressure is right. And of course they can solidify (freeze) if cooled to the appropriate degree. A property which is not without its geological significance is that of surface tension, where the surface of the liquid appears like tightly stretched skin. This allows some light objects, e.g. insects, to rest on the liquid surface and it draws liquids into spheres or drops (rain, etc.).

One property of liquids, especially of water, of immense geological importance is the power to dissolve substances. This in effect amounts to breaking up the molecules of the dissolved material into atomic groups or ions which then wander around between the water molecules.

Solids have definite volumes, weights and shapes. Their derivatives are not very different from those of liquids, but solids do vary in their compressibility. Rocks are difficult to compress. Many solids have remarkably regular forms with definite patterns of flat surfaces and angles – they appear crystalline. Heat a solid and it may melt, and even at temperatures below melting point some solids evaporate. Snow and mothballs both do this; so do some minerals.

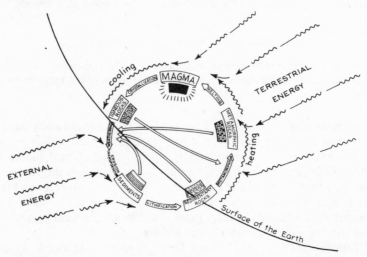

The rock cycle: how matter may change its character and role during geological time. If no interruption occurs the cycle will continue round and round in a few score million years to a few hundred million years. To keep the cycle moving energy is needed from both the sun and from inside the earth.

The three states of matter are illustrated by our general concept of the earth as a planet with a thin skin of gas on the outside (the atmosphere), an irregular layer of liquid below that (the hydrosphere), and innermost the solid rock ball (the lithosphere). Of course the earth is not quite so simple and it is the way in which solar radiation, gravity and the radioactive energy within the lithosphere have kept these layers moving and reacting with one another that has made the earth a truly vital planet.

MINERALS

For the moment we must leave aside the gases and liquids. The nature of solids, however, is very well illustrated by the study of minerals. Minerals are solid, make up rocks, and so constitute much the greater part of the planet. Some of them came into existence during the earliest stages of the formation of the earth.

Although mineralogists might quibble about the exact wording, a convenient definition of minerals is that they are solid products of

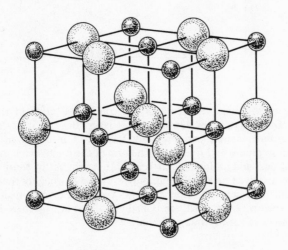

The neat stacking of sodium ions, Na^+, and chlorine ions, Cl^-, in sodium chloride, $NaCl$, results from their electrical charges cancelling out under the rule that opposite charges attract and like charges repel. Our diagram shows these ions pulled apart from one another so that we can see the bonding. In reality the ions are packed close to one another like so many bull's eyes in a jar.

nature, each having a definite chemical composition and which could have existed on earth before life began. So they must be chemical elements or compounds and they are not just random mixtures of elements. The atoms making up each mineral have definite ratios to one another. We can express this in the chemical formula for each mineral. Some 2000 different minerals are known.

There is some difference of opinion as to whether or not the naturally occurring hydrocarbon compounds (such as oil and coal) and other organically produced substances can be minerals in the strict sense of the word. One certainly has to regard them as *earth materials* since they are produced naturally in the crust of the earth or at its surface.

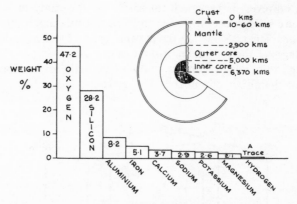

Abundance of the major elements in the continental crust of the earth. The *crust* of the earth is its thin outermost layer. Beneath it lies a second layer, the *mantle,* denser and probably formed of iron and magnesium silicates and sulphides and free iron. The *core* of the earth seems to have an outer liquid part and an inner solid kernel. It is thought to consist of iron with a little dissolved nickel. We can only examine thoroughly the crust on the continents and here the evidence shows that most of it is made up of a very few elements. As we shall see (Chapter 2), this is why there is such a limited number of rock-forming minerals.

CRYSTALS

One of the properties of minerals to attract early man's attention must have been their smooth surfaces, reflecting light as do facets on gems. Minerals characteristically occur as crystals, with their smooth flat surfaces more or less developed to give regular geometrical shapes. There are almost no limits to the size of crystals. They may be microscopic or they may be enormous. In the Haliburton area of Ontario, crystals of apatite occur as big as logs; Brazilian quartz crystals weigh several hundred pounds. Biggest of all crystals are the feldspars: in Norway, for example, crystals around 2m by 3·5m by 8m may be seen in old quarries. Crystals grow by the addition of uniform layers of atoms depending upon the kind of mineral and on the kind of carrier or solvent around it. But large size has its disadvantages and the would-be mineralogist soon discovers that the smaller the crystal the better its shape, and the better the shape the easier it may be to identify the exact type and composition of the mineral. Many crystals have an obvious symmetry, presenting the same appearance to several directions. Those popular crystalline substances, sugar and salt, both have symmetry, possessing square crystal faces and forming white cubic crystals. Other crystalline materials possess symmetries less easily recognized. When crystals are to be analysed we need to know what the symmetry is: it is a real indication of the mineral's structure. Crystal symmetry (and shape) is, in fact, important in classifying minerals, and it has long been known that, despite their seemingly endless variety, crystal symmetry does fall into a small number of basic categories – the crystal systems. Some mineralogists incline to six, others prefer seven systems.

Early in this century the idea that crystals had an orderly arrangement of atoms to build up their remarkable shapes was put to the test by a physicist, Professor Max von Laue. He examined crystals by putting them in an X-ray beam and recording how the beam was dispersed on to a photographic plate. The experiments were highly successful. It appeared that each different crystal produced its own distinctive regular pattern of surrounding spots on the plate. This surely indicated that as the X-rays passed through the crystal they were bent by a regular arrangement of atoms, or ions. When crystals of the same shape but different compositions were used, similar though not identical patterns showed up. With a bit more ingenuity it was shown that these patterns could be used to identify a crystal's lattice-work of ions or atoms and that the relative sizes of the ions and their spacing could be measured. Crystal shape was seen to depend on the way in which the atoms are linked and spaced in what we call the crystal lattice structure.

Before this method of analysis was invented, minerals were analysed in various ways, nearly all of which involved partially destroying them.

X-ray portraits and patterns. *Above,* the orderly arrangement of atoms in the crystals of the mineral pyrite (page 48) in which each large spot, an atom of iron, is grouped with two small spots, the atoms of sulphur, and the iron atoms are equidistant from one another. *Below,* in the mineral marcasite (page 48) the iron atoms also link with two sulphur atoms but are differently spaced. Magnification over two million diameters. (After photographs by M. J. Buerger).

These methods could give the chemical composition of a mineral but nothing else, and of course the crystal structure was never revealed. X-ray work changed all that. X-rays do not harm the crystal structure and they show that it is a fundamental property of every mineral.

Mineralogists were now on the trail of the *unit cell* – the smallest possible unit of a crystal. They supposed that it would be a regular arrangement of atoms held together by electrical forces – a building block from which all crystals of the same composition would be formed – and of course it would be too small to be seen. From mineral to mineral the size and shape of these unit cells or building blocks would vary, depending on the kinds, sizes and numbers of atoms

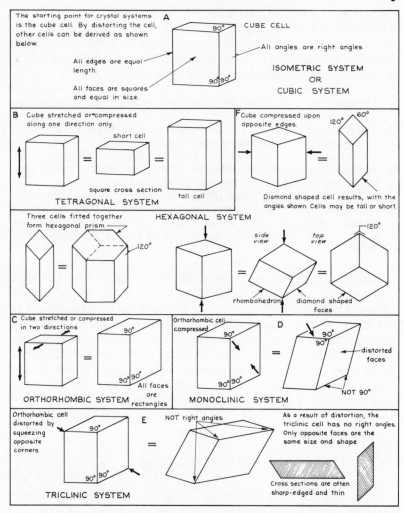

The crystal systems. Despite the many shapes crystals exhibit, there are really only six basic patterns to which the shapes are related. Starting from the very well-behaved regular cube we can pass to other shapes where the square faces are progressively replaced by others less regular, such as rectangles and rhomboids. (After J. Sinkankas, 1965).

present and on their arrangement. All this has been confirmed. It was also found that in building up crystals, the unit cells fit together very snugly so that no spaces are left between them. So perfectly do they fit that only six basic forms or cell shapes are possible, and these correspond to the six accepted basic crystal systems.

1. *Isometric*: units are cubes; all edges equal in length and perpendicular to one another.
2. *Tetragonal*: at each corner of the basic form three edges at right angles to one another but only two of equal length.
3. *Orthorhombic*: three edges at right angles, all of different lengths.
4. *Monoclinic*: at each corner edges all of different lengths; two at right angles and one inclined to the plane of the other two.
5. *Triclinic*: at each corner edges all different lengths and not at right angles.
6. *Hexagonal*: at each corner two edges equal making angles of 60 and 120 degrees to each other; third edge is at right angles to them and of different length. Three of these units fit together to make a regular hexagonal prism.

We can see crystals made up of these faces fairly often, but more commonly we find crystals which have other faces too. A little research shows that these additional faces are arranged not haphazardly but in a constant angular relationship to the others. This too is determined by the unit cells. A good comparison can be drawn by stacking (perfectly orthorhombic) bricks with like edges together. They can make faces at right angles or at other angles by varying the number used. 'Perfect' crystals have corresponding faces all of the same size, and they have, of course, the most regular internal structure.

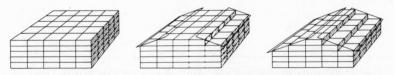

Crystals and unit cells. The simple orthorhombic house brick can be piled into stacks of various shapes by placing each brick face next to a similar face. The stacks can be cubic or of another shape depending on how the bricks are laid in rows. By adding or subtracting rows we can make apparently sloping surfaces, and the angular relationship of these surfaces to the vertical wall of the pile and the flat top layer is constant. Crystal faces may be produced by the piling of unit cells in this manner.

Crystal Symmetry

What we have seen so far leads to the observation that crystals are basically symmetrical arrangements of ions. This symmetry can be described quite simply by referring to three elemental features, *planes* of symmetry, *axes* of symmetry, and *centres* of symmetry. Crystals are classified on this basis.

The possible combinations of axes, planes and centres of symmetry in crystals give us thirty-two *crystal classes*, including an odd one with no symmetry at all. One might now reasonably ask why there are so many crystal classes if there are only six (or seven) fundamental forms. The variety arises from the different arrangements of atoms in the unit cell. Different arrangements of atoms give different geometry to the faces, and different external symmetry of the crystals follows.

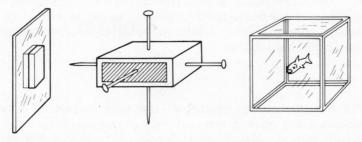

Planes, axes and centres of symmetry. A *plane* of symmetry divides the crystal into two parts which are mirror images of each other. A plane of symmetry may be illustrated by holding half an object – a brick, an orange, or a crystal – against a mirror. The reflected image seems to restore the missing half and the mirror corresponds to the plane. An *axis* of symmetry is an axis through the centre of the crystal such that rotation about it repeats sets of faces a number of times in a complete rotation. An *axis* of symmetry is thus an imaginary line passing through the middle of similar faces or edges on opposite sides of the crystal. A matchbox pierced by knitting needles is a good analogy. A *centre* of symmetry exists if for every face there is a similar face parallel to it and at the opposite side of the centre. A *centre* of symmetry is the point within the crystal from where the view of any one of a pair of crystal faces is the same as the view of the other – like a goldfish-eye view of the sides of a full tank seen from the middle of a cubic tank.

Colour

In addition to crystal form the characters of minerals which would attract early man's attention – and ours – would be colour and lustre. The brilliant hues of some minerals have always been highly prized; yet even today we do not in every case really understand the reasons for the colours. Many minerals have colours which vary with their chemical composition, but most minerals are composed of elements which produce no characteristic colour or which are colourless. Colour seems largely to be due in these cases to tiny impurities. Such traces of 'foreign' elements in a crystal may damage the lattice structure and so cause it to absorb certain wavelengths of light which would otherwise pass through.

Though colour is often a good clue to a mineral's identity, it can be deceptive and should never be used alone. The *streak* of a mineral may help. This is the colour of its powder, and it may be very different from that of the whole mineral. When scratched or rubbed on an abrasive surface, a streak of powder may be left behind. Black haematite, for example, has a red streak.

Lustre

The ability to shine – to reflect light – is an attractive property of many minerals and it gives us two convenient groups – metallic and non-metallic minerals. Metallic minerals reflect light, so that they have a generally shiny or brilliant appearance, and they are opaque. On the other hand, most non-metallic minerals reflect little light from their surfaces: they are pale coloured and allow light to penetrate. The degree to which they are transparent is related to the lustre minerals possess, and this in turn is related to the substance's ability to bend light passing through it. This power to bend from its original path a beam of light as it passes through the mineral is called its refractive index. It is an important property, useful in determining the nature of minerals; by measuring refractive indices very accurately, jewellers are able to identify gems.

Once again we can trace the origin of physical properties back to atomic character and arrangement in crystal structure. A high refractive index and therefore a high lustre are found both in minerals containing heavy metals and in those where the atoms are very tightly packed. That hardest of minerals, diamond, is an admirable example of the latter.

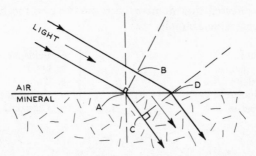

Refraction. The speed at which light travels depends upon *what it is travelling through*. When light enters a mineral, or a piece of glass, or water, it is bent or *refracted* towards the plane perpendicular to the surface. In the same time that light travels from B to D in the air it also travels from A to C in the mineral. The ratio BD : AC which is the velocity of light in air divided by the velocity of light in the mineral is called the *refractive index*. Thus a medium with a high refractive index allows light to travel only at slow speed; the higher the velocity through the medium the lower the refractive index. For example, the refractive index of water is 1.33, crown glass 1.53, diamond 2.42.

Type of lustre	Examples	Degree of lustre
brilliant (adamantine)	diamond	High
vitreous (glassy)	quartz	High
resinous (resin)	sulphur	High
greasy	talc	High
pearly	calcite	High
silky (fibrous)	gypsum	Low

Hardness

Diamonds are today prized perhaps more for their hardness and consequent use in industry than as gemstones. Whereas in stone-age technology flint would serve, the modern world needs hard metals and minerals, especially those resistant to wear and tear, such as diamonds. Hardness is a product of the dense packing of atoms in the structure of a mineral, so it may be suspected when a mineral has a high lustre. To measure degrees of hardness, the Austrian mineralogist Friedrich Mohs (1773–1839) drew up the scale most widely used today.

Minerals are referred to a number corresponding to the hardness of an easily recognizable example, viz:

Soft | 1. Talc | 6. Feldspar
        | 2. Gypsum | 7. Quartz
        | 3. Calcite | 8. Topaz
        | 4. Fluorite | 9. Corundum
        | 5. Apatite   *Hard* | 10. Diamond

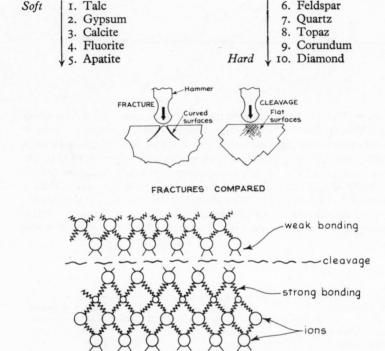

FRACTURES COMPARED

Types of fracture. When hit with a hammer a crystal (or rock) may suffer a fracture, seen as a rough or curved surface. Many minerals, however, will break into well defined pieces bounded by flat regular faces. Such flat fracture is *cleavage* and the cleavage planes pass through the weakest bonds in the atomic structure of the mineral.

Cleavage

Although minerals may have several different kinds of crystal face, on breaking some show a remarkable tendency to split along planes parallel to only one or two such faces. In some instances this tendency, cleavage, is not parallel to an actual crystal face but only to the plane in which one possibly could exist. The angles on the faces of cleaved fragments are constant and diagnostic while in unbroken minerals they can be seen between parallel cracks or faint lines. Cleavage can be explained by looking again into the crystal structure. The atoms so regularly positioned in the lattice are held together by electrical charges or bonds. The strength of this bonding varies between different types of atom and with crystallographic direction. Where the bonding is weakest the layers of atoms are most easily parted, and because it is a planar feature in most minerals they tend to split along planes at right angles to the weakest bonding force. Since the arrangement of layers within the crystal controls its form it is easy to understand how cleavage and crystal form are related.

The number, quality and directions of cleavage planes are important in mineral identification and are constant no matter whether one examines a giant crystal or a microscopic fragment.

Specific Gravity

Quite a number of minerals are heavy in the hand. They have a high density, and by comparing this to that of water we say they have a high specific gravity. Most rock-forming minerals, such as feldspar, have specific gravities between 2.50 and 2.75, but those of most of the metallic ore minerals are rather higher. These metallic minerals have a

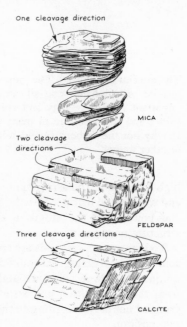

One cleavage direction

MICA

Two cleavage directions

FELDSPAR

Three cleavage directions

CALCITE

Cleavage and structure. Cleavage is an important feature in the identification of many minerals. Some minerals have one cleavage, others two, yet others have three.

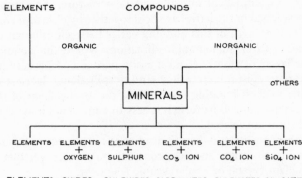

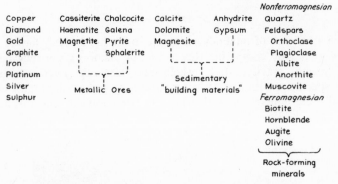

The mineral family tree. The more common minerals are oxides, sulphides, carbonates, sulphates, and silicates. The silicates have perhaps the most important role in geology and are the main rock-forming minerals. The oxides and sulphides are in many cases associated with heat and volcanic activity but the carbonates and sulphates are usually precipitated from sea or other waters.

high lustre, and the association of the two properties is a well-known and widespread feature. Specific gravity then may be related to the type and bonding of the atoms in the mineral. We are back to crystal structure once again.

To summarize, minerals are special combinations of elements in the solid state, occurring naturally and with a diagnostic composition, a unique crystalline structure and the physical properties that result from the composition and structure. The common minerals can be grouped not only according to their crystal symmetry but also by their composition.

PLATE I. The minerals of Moh's Scale: calcite (3) is at centre, and then from the top in clockwise order are corundum (9), quartz (7), apatite (5), diamond (10), gypsum (2), talc (1), topaz (8), fluorspar (4), feldspar (6).

PLATE 2. Distinctive mineral forms are commonly very simple, as with calcite (6), pyrite (striated) (5), selenite or gypsum (4), mica (1), garnet (3) and tourmaline (2). About natural size.

CHAPTER 2

THE ESSENTIAL FEW:
ROCK-FORMING MINERALS

IN this chapter we shall look at quartz and a few other minerals that outweigh all the others in their abundance and importance in geology. As we have just seen, the materials from which all kinds of rocks are made are the minerals, yet many rocks seem at first sight to have no crystalline structure at all: however, when a very thin sliver of such a rock is examined under a microscope it may present quite a different picture. We see that it is build up entirely of crystals, or that scattered throughout it are tiny chunks of crystalline substance. Having seen many such thin slices of rock, the geologist recognizes that even in widely differing kinds of material certain minerals occur many times more abundantly than others. They are aptly named *rock-forming minerals*, and it would be nice if such important things as these were simple to understand. But they are not: apart from quartz and one or two others, they are complicated silicates of aluminium, iron, calcium, potassium, sodium and magnesium. Sometimes a few other elements are present as well.

That so few minerals can make up such an enormous variety of rock types is perhaps a little difficult to grasp, but one may think of rocks as mixtures or aggregates of different minerals. Just as the cakes and bread in a baker's window are composed of various combinations of flour, sugar, fruit, eggs, cream, and so on, rocks are natural confections of minerals. We might say the baker's window had breads, biscuits and cakes. Geology has three kinds of rocks – each formed in a basically different way. *Igneous* rocks are those that have formed from once-molten matter called *magma*. The first solid crust of the earth was made of igneous rocks and in the millions of years since then many other rocks have been derived from those first igneous formations.

This has come about by weathering and rotting of the igneous rocks, producing new material or sediment. Sediments accumulating in the sea or other hollows in the earth's surface have eventually become *sedimentary* rocks. Both igneous and sedimentary rocks may suffer great changes when they become deeply buried in the earth's crust. Compressed, and perhaps scorched or heated by terrestrial heat, they are *metamorphosed* or changed, largely by recrystallizing, into *metamorphic* rocks. But in all these rocks we may find the same kinds of rock-forming minerals. It is what has happened to them that gives us the different kinds of rocks.

Modern scientific methods can be used to examine these rocks and minerals down to their basic atomic structure. The techniques are complicated but they can be employed to analyse 'artificial' minerals made in the laboratory, using very high pressures and high temperatures. By melting minerals together under high pressure in the laboratory and then slowly cooling the mixture, rock materials resembling those in nature can be produced. What emerges from all this is a general understanding that rock and mineral composition and structure (coarsely crystalline, glassy, or microcrystalline, for example) depend on not only the kinds and proportions of elements present but also on the temperature and pressure in the earth where they form.

Before we look at the internal structures of the rock-forming minerals and how they are produced it is necessary to make a quick survey of the general properties that the most common of them have. In almost any igneous rock one will find that the minerals fall into a number of natural categories. These are quartz, feldspars, and white micas (sometimes called *felsics*, or rather clumsily, the *non-ferromagnesians*), and dark minerals called *ferromagnesians* because they are rich in iron and magnesium, with perhaps metallic ores such as magnetite or pyrite.

QUARTZ

Quartz is a simple substance, silicon dioxide SiO_2. It is very widespread and can take very different forms. It is usually thought of as belonging to the hexagonal system and, when pure, is transparent and quite colourless like glass. In fact, this variety is the much-prized 'rock crystal'. Most quartz, however, has some degree of colour due to impurities. The fully formed crystals are six-sided prisms with pyramidal ends, but in most rocks these have little chance to grow. The best crystals come from large veins where they once grew in hot fluids. Quartz crystals have no cleavage but may show fine parallel striations on their faces. A steel knife blade will scratch quartz only with much difficulty; this helps distinguish the mineral from calcite which is softer. On Mohs' scale the hardnesses are 7 and 3 respectively. Quartz is an inactive mineral in the sense that it dissolves in water only very slowly indeed, and little else makes any impression on it. Most of the quartz we see is detrital – weathered and worn fragments derived from crystalline rocks and veins.

Varieties of quartz may have beautiful colours and are regarded as semi-precious or ornamental stones. Jasper and carnelian are red, chalcedony is white or yellowish. These stones are made up of finely crystalline material tinged with a little iron oxide. Opal is a semi-precious form with a vitreous to irridescent lustre.

Quartz has many uses in modern technology and is important, as sand, as a source of glassmaking material, as an abrasive and hard substance and as a component in electrical equipment.

FELDSPARS

By far the most abundant minerals in the crust of the earth are the feldspars. They are a complicated group, silicates of aluminium in most cases with one or two other metals, and sodium, potassium or calcium. In most veins of giant crystals (pegmatites) feldspar is present, but in the common igneous rocks the varieties of feldspar may be in crystals too small to be identified by the naked eye. Some rocks can be seen to contain small, whitish, nuggety crystals of *orthoclase* feldspar (potassium-rich) and/or flat platelets or laths of *plagioclase* feldspar (the sodium- and calcium-rich varieties). These are, in fact, the two major kinds of feldspars. Both are whitish, or they may be pink, grey, bluish, or even yellow. A few feldspars have exotic colours: amazon stone is a beautiful green.

When they are in perfect crystals feldspars occur in a squat prismatic form, belong to the monoclinic and triclinic systems, and are easily

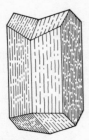 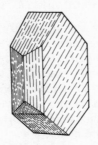 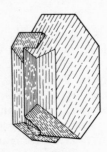

Feldspars, some of the most important rock-forming minerals, are not frequently seen as well-shaped crystals. They are commonly twinned as is the distinctive plagioclase on the left and the orthoclase on the right. The single orthoclase crystal form is shown in the middle.

recognized. They have two sets of good cleavage, meeting at, or almost at, a right angle. Hardness is 6 in Mohs' scale and there is a bright or dull, often nacreous, lustre. The twinning that the crystals may show is one of the most readily recognizable characteristics of feldspar. It can be seen on the cleavage surfaces of the larger crystals, and the kind of twinning will indicate whether an orthoclase or a plagioclase feldspar is present.

Orthoclase feldspars show twinning by an uneven brightness of the adjacent halves on a cleavage face. Plagioclase feldspars have a repeated twinning in thin slivers; some twinning is too fine to see except with a microscope.

One or two varieties of calcium-rich feldspar, such as *labradorite*, show a marvellous array of peacock colours in an irridescence that changes as the angle of light changes on a crystal face. Other dark feldspars are very conspicuous in some coarsely crystalline rocks from Norway which are popular ornamental stones.

Feldspars, both orthoclase and plagioclase, may occur in the same rock, but plagioclase seems to be less abundant in the company of quartz. However, both kinds are prone to chemical attack in the rock, even before crystallization was completed, and in the upper reaches of the crust where free water can help the action along. Feldspars soon become rather dull and porcellanous-looking on exposure, and they ultimately break down into a fine white clay.

Decomposed by vapours deep in the crust, orthoclase feldspar gives rise to *kaolinite*, china clay, a fine white clay mineral. It is much in demand in the pottery, chemical and paper industries.

MICAS, CHLORITE, TALC

This group of substances is easy to identify because the members are all so soft. Micas are platy minerals, rather elastic and glittery. They split easily along cleavage planes into very thin rather transparent layers. White mica, *muscovite*, was once used in place of glass in windows in Russia, hence its name. *Biotite* is a black mica, and *phlogopite* is brown. Mica sheets are produced by cleaving the crystals, so a hexagonal outline tends to suggest the hexagonal system, but in fact these minerals are monoclinic.

Chlorite may look somewhat platy and green. It is soft and rather soapy to the touch, but in nature it generally occurs in such small pieces, flakes and scales, that it is difficult to identify by touch. Chlorite seems

Micas are variously coloured or black shiny
flakey minerals with characteristic six-sided
flat crystals.

locally to be a decomposition product, commonly arising from the
alteration of one of the other ferromagnesian minerals such as augite.
It belongs to the monoclinic system but cleaves into hexagonal flakes
which may be rather flexible.

Talc is a very soft, soapy and massive material of similar origin. It is
usually found in massive forms known as *steatite* or soapstone which
has various shades of red, grey, green and white. Talc has an enormous
number of uses from tailor's chalk to electrical gear.

AMPHIBOLES

Amphiboles, pyroxenes and *olivine* are the common ferromagnesian
minerals, rich in iron, magnesium and perhaps calcium and other
metals. Sometimes they are also called 'mafic' minerals; all are dark in
colour and rather heavy.

Hornblende is the most often encountered of the amphiboles, and is
fairly typical of this group. It forms shining blade-like prisms and has
two cleavages at about 56 degrees to each other, which give long,
narrow, sharp-edged splinters. In colour it may be green, brown or
black, but some varieties are pale, or even white. Hornblende is found
in many granite-like rocks and in veins associated with them. Hornblende and the common amphiboles crystallize in the monoclinic
system. All, however, have their cleavage sets and prism faces at 124
degrees to one another.

PYROXENES

Like amphiboles, these minerals are common in some igneous rocks
and they resemble amphiboles in appearance and hardness, 6 on

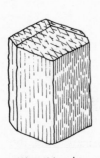
Hornblende

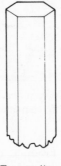
Tourmaline

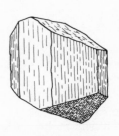
Augite

Important and common ferromagnesian rock-forming minerals are horn-blende, augite and tourmaline. The first two are much more abundant than tourmaline and their crystals less commonly found in veins, where very splendid tourmalines may occur.

Mohs' scale. *Augite* is the common pyroxene, occurring in stubby crystals belonging to the monoclinic system. It also has less lustre than hornblende and has two sets of cleavage almost at right angles to one another. Augite usually occurs in dark igneous rocks such as basalt. When basalts decompose it is in many cases the augite crystals that alter to chlorite and other materials first.

OLIVINE

Fresh olivine is not easy to find, but it does occur in basaltic rocks. There it is commonly present as *phenocrysts*, isolated larger crystals set in a fine-grained matrix. It is rather an unstable silicate, hard, glassy and greenish when fresh but dulled and of lighter colour where it begins to combine with water. Olivine belongs to the orthorhombic system and may occur as small globose crystals. The semi-precious stone *peridot* is a variety of olivine.

MAGNETITE, ILMENITE

Most igneous rocks and many sedimentary rocks contain grains of one or both of these minerals. They are iron oxides, heavy and opaque. Magnetite can be picked out of crushed igneous rock or extracted from sands by a magnet. Ilmenite is an iron titanium oxide.

SILICATE STRUCTURES

More than 90% of all rock-forming minerals are silicates, and silicates have some special properties of their own. The essential part in a silicate mineral is the silicon-oxygen tetrahedron. Without this there would be no silicates, and it must have been one of the first groupings of atoms to form as the earth cooled from its molten state. We may use a simple, if unlikely, analogy when thinking of this tetrahedron – a ping-pong ball of silicon surrounded by four footballs of oxygen. The oxygen atoms are larger than the silicon atom jammed between them and they have together an electric charge of −8. The silicon atom has an electric charge of +4, so between them they give the tetrahedron a charge of −4.

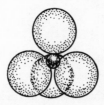

The 'ultimate particle' in rock-building components, the one atom of silicon and four atoms of oxygen which together are the silicon tetrahedron necessary in all the silicate minerals (90% of earth's crust).

In silicate minerals these tetrahedra are joined to ions in regular fashion. The way they do this and the combinations in which the other ions join up, control the chemical and physical character of the minerals – a theme suggested in Chapter 1.

Just how the tetrahedra and ions link up varies from single tetrahedra alternating with positively charged metal ions to chains, sheets and three-dimensional structures.

Single chain structures are thought of as shown on page 40. Each silicon atom shares two of its bonded oxygen atoms with a neighbour and has two atoms just to itself. The arrangement produces a pretty strong chain and the chains themselves are in turn bonded to one another by metallic ions with a positive charge. As it happens, the bonds between the metal ions are not so strong as those linking the tetrahedra to one another. When a stress is applied they give way – these planes of weakness allow cleavage to develop in a mineral and it is, of course, parallel to the silicon-oxygen tetrahedra chains.

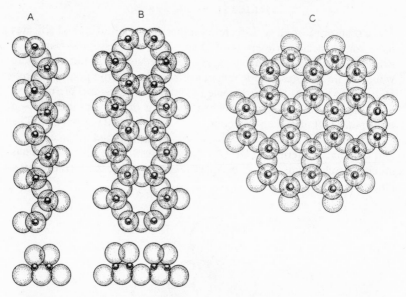

A, Single chains of silicon tetrahedra are found in the pyroxene rock-forming minerals. B, Double chains of silicon tetrahedra occur in other great groups of ferromagnesian rock-forming minerals, the amphiboles. C, In the clay minerals and micas the tetrahedra group into sheets or layers and alternate with metallic elements. It is easy to see how a very dominant cleavage parallel to the sheets results from this.

Augite has just such a crystalline structure, based on single chains of tetrahedra joined together by ions of iron, calcium and magnesium. Its cleavage planes lie almost at right angles to one another.

Double chains are formed when alternate tetrahedra share *three* of their oxygen atoms with others. The result is pictured above. In these cases the chains are bonded together not only by ions of iron and magnesium (the usual agents in the ferromagnesian minerals) but also by calcium, aluminium, sodium or other elements. In the case of the amphiboles such as the common *hornblende* it is this arrangement with calcium, aluminium and, in some, sodium helping out that gives the mineral the property that distinguishes it from augite – cleavage planes meeting at about 56 degrees.

The next complicated formation in the parade of these tetrahedra is that of continuous sheets (above). Here each silicon atom shares three of its oxygen atoms with neighbouring silicon atoms. An open pattern is produced, rather like wire netting with the oxygen odd-man out, the unshared atoms sticking up above the others. No minerals better show this kind of structure than the micas. In biotite, for example, there are such sheets of silicon-oxygen tetrahedra in pairs, with the projecting unattached oxygen atoms facing in towards ions of iron and magnesium. The flat opposite sides of these sheets are bonded weakly to positive ions of potassium. When one splits biotite into flakes it is the potassium links that are weak and break. Hence the wonderfully flat thin (cleavage) fragments.

White mica, muscovite, has a structure like biotite. Each pair of tetrahedra sheets is firmly held together by bonds to ions of aluminium. The puny bonds which sandwich potassium ions between the double sheets are more easily broken. This is where the cleavage develops.

FRAMEWORKS FOR FELDSPARS

The silicate structures we have discussed so far are not very complicated. Now we need to look at more elaborate affairs. Feldspars are silicates: they have silicon-oxygen tetrahedra arranged in a three-dimensional network, like the steel skeleton of a skyscraper or giant office block.

In these constructions, however, the oxygen ions are all shared, but a strange thing has happened. When there should be silicon ions, in places they have been replaced by aluminium ions. It is as though there had not been enough silicon to go round so some of the oxygen atoms ganged-up on available aluminium ions, or aluminium ions had intruded into the tetrahedra. These newcomers are just a little bigger than the silicon ions and they have an electric charge of $3+$. The silicons chased out had a charge of $4+$ so there seems to be a single negative charge from the oxygens left unconnected. Such a state of affairs is not permitted. An invasion of potassium, sodium or calcium ions is called in to neutralize the spare positive charge. There is nearly always a supply of these ions waiting to answer the call from the feldspar structure. What is interesting is that it is rare for only one of these outsiders to monopolize the field. Usually two of them are present. When they are sodium and calcium, a plagioclase feldspar results; when it is potassium (and it manages to keep the other two out), orthoclase feldspar is formed. What decides which of these ions gets into the feldspar structure and in what proportions?

The answer in the case of feldspar is really much the same as for most of the other rock-forming minerals. Briefly, it has to do with the temperature and pressure at which the crystals form. At low temperatures the atoms in a solid material tend to behave quietly and stand in their prescribed positions. When the material is heated the atoms begin to shove and push about until their order is quite gone. At this stage the material melts or vaporizes. As temperatures drop the atoms calm down, so to speak, and get back in line so that the solid state is regained. If we change not only temperature but also pressure we find that the heat at which melting takes place can be drastically altered. Another influence tending to lower melting points is the presence of small amounts of water.

In the earth where temperatures and pressures can be very high, the molten material can be kept very hot for enormous periods of time. All sorts of things can affect or alter the temperature and/or the pressure of the molten rock to cause interruptions in the settling out and growth of crystals there. To some extent we can experiment in the laboratory to reproduce the conditions and materials that occur in the earth, but it is not easy. We can only make intelligent guesses as to what really happens deep in the crust of the earth where some of our igneous rocks are created.

The hot material deep down is a complicated mixture of molten silicates, oxides, sulphides and other substances, including water

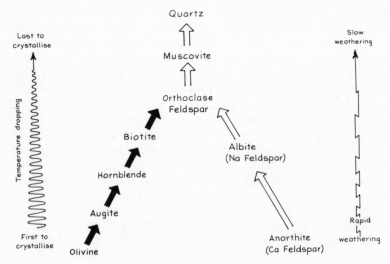

The crystallization series.

vapour and gas. Volcanic lava gives off steam and gas as it comes up out of the earth. The molten material is what we term a *melt* and its *components* arrange themselves into ions and crystal structures according to the heat and pressure around them.

Imagine a melt of silicates at high temperature. As it cools some crystals form and so some material has been removed from the 'liquid' of the melt. What is left behind is now of a different composition from the original melt. If the whole is suddenly chilled, the crystals and non-crystalline melt are all frozen. When we analyse them, the crystals may show a rather different composition from the glass that was the liquid in the melt. The same melt suddenly frozen at a lower temperature would perhaps show that the first-formed crystals had reacted with the fluid around them and were being replaced by crystalline matter that came out of solution at a lower temperature.

In the case of feldspars, they crystallize from melts at high temperatures as shown opposite. When potassium or sodium are present, orthoclase feldspar is produced; when sodium and calcium are there, plagioclase feldspar crystallizes. If we can find the proportion of these

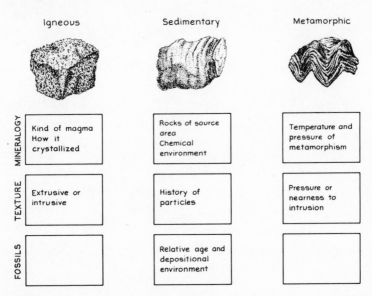

The mineralogy and the texture of a rock are clues as to its nature and origin. (After Press and Siever).

elements present in a feldspar we are on the way to knowing how hot it was when the mineral was formed.

Other minerals may tell us much the same story and we know nowadays what temperatures and pressures are needed before most of the common rock-forming minerals appear. Last of all to appear as a melt crystallizes are the metallic oxides, such as magnetite, and quartz. Magnetite, however, may crystallize at an early stage too. So it seems that the minerals with least complicated silicate structures may form first and that, as temperatures drop, the minerals with more complicated patterns of tetrahedra form. The pushing and shoving of atoms at higher temperatures seems to keep the tetrahedra from linking up very much. As they quieten down so they collect into more complicated arrangements and are content to share more of their oxygen atoms. When all is crystallized or 'set' there may be some silicon-oxygen tetrahedra and metallic oxides left over. By that time, however, the rock-forming minerals have lived up to their name and have crystallized to produce a rock.

CHAPTER 3

ALL BRIGHT AND SHINING:
THE METALLIC ORES

THE stone-age man who dropped a cherished, brightly coloured mineral into his fire must have been dismayed at his loss. Raking over the ashes, however, he may have found that his coloured stone had turned into a heavy lump of metal, reduced from its mineral form by the heat of the fire. Perhaps it was not such a loss after all, for there were all sorts of immediate uses for the metal. Today the search for metallic ores is a highly developed and extensive business on which hundreds of thousands of pounds are spent every year. No longer is it a matter of grubbing a few nuggets out of the ground, but a search to find the biggest deposits possible. We are able now to extract metal from ores that yield less than 1%, but to make it worthwhile the ore has to be in many hundreds of thousands of tons.

In this book we can deal with only a very few of the metallic ores that are common, interesting and are (or were) economically important. Britain seems to have had more than its fair share of metallic ores and they are by no means exhausted. Recently big discoveries have been made in Ireland, but the largest deposits of the minerals we need so much in modern industry are, for the most part, found in the ancient rocks of Canada, Africa, Australia and Russia. They are no longer worked by lone miners and prospectors but by international mining companies. The minerals we shall look at in this chapter can still be found in many parts of the British Isles. They are the minerals that the old prospectors sought and which today the mining company's geologist still seeks as an indication of hidden ore bodies.

There are three major groups of minerals which include most of the ores we have been talking about – native or uncombined elements, oxides and sulphides. Other less important ores occur as carbonates, sulphates, phosphates, and so on.

NATIVE ELEMENTS

These are rare indeed, since they are generally occurrences of metals that have not been combined with 'metal hungry' elements such as oxygen (and sulphur). The list of those one might find is small: copper, gold, carbon (graphite), iron, silver and sulphur. There are nearly twenty other elements that occur naturally (native). One of the most valued is carbon in the form of diamond; it is of course very rare, very hard, and known in only a few places on earth.

COPPER is one of the most common of the native elements but it is not often found in Britain. It occurs in jagged or lacy lumps, branches and shards, and in its rare crystal form it makes up rough cubes, octahedra and dodecahedra. Of course when it is fresh it looks like copper. It is soft and heavy and was hammered into tools by the North American Indians before the white man came. In most places where it occurs there are also the black, blue and green copper compound minerals to be found. These usually lie near to or within large parent masses of copper sulphide ore which are in veins and in sedimentary or basaltic rocks.

SILVER is a most beautiful native element, commonly occurring as rough masses or fine wire and rarely as cubes, octahedra and dodecahedra. It has a characteristic brilliant colour and lustre, is rather soft and very heavy. Native silver is known from many parts of the world, where it occurs with oxide and sulphide minerals and basaltic rocks. Localities in Europe, particularly Norway and Germany, have long been famous for the mineral, but specimens are very rare these days.

GOLD needs almost no description. It is the yellow, soft, very heavy element found in lodes and veins, and as grains in sands ('placers') from many parts of the world. Gold is sometimes found mixed with small amounts of silver. In its crystal shape it may be an octahedron but, for the most part, gold occurs as composite octahedral crystals, as thin plates and as cubes. As a vein mineral it is associated with quartz and sulphides around granitic intrusions or in metamorphic rocks. The big goldfields of the world are famous, but gold has also been found in Cornwall, North and Central Wales, and Scotland. Even nowadays people think it worth while to keep prospecting for it in these parts.

IRON is not found native in Britain, but several places in Europe, especially Germany, have yielded small nuggets of this metal from basaltic rocks.

ARSENIC occurs in small nodular masses or crusts, in association with other minerals, at Saltash in Cornwall and in France and Germany. It has a metallic lustre, is heavy and soft, and leaves a white streak. When heated it may turn into dense white fumes, and of course it is *poisonous*.

SULPHUR is one of the prettiest of minerals when it occurs as fine orthorhombic tabular or pyramidal crystals with a rather glassy yellow or orange appearance. It is soft, and it burns to give off acrid fumes like those of a newly struck match.

CARBÓN. Not many of us ever find a diamond, at least in its native state, but it is such a remarkable mineral that we ought to mention it here. It is the hardest substance known, a pure crystalline form of carbon, an element which we also find as dull, soft graphite. Diamond crystals are most commonly octahedra; cubes are rare. The most valued diamonds are transparent, clear and colourless, but many pale clear shades are known, and there are even almost black types. Although it is hard, diamond is also brittle, and it breaks with a conchoidal fracture.

In several parts of the world diamonds are found as pebbles or grains of sands, gravels or sandstones. They have been washed there from 'blue ground', the weathered part of certain kinds of igneous rocks. Africa and Brazil are well known for their 'blue ground' and alluvial banks, and diamonds are sought now in the off-shore sediments which have been swept off the ancient land. Being so hard and resistant, diamonds survive all manner of geological rough treatment, but they are usually reduced to less than 3 mm in diameter.

We think that this gemstone, the only one that is a native element, crystallizes from a melt under very great pressure indeed and so originates at enormous depths within the earth.

Graphite is a contrast indeed to diamond, but it is the same element in a different form. Soft, grey-black and in thin tabular hexagonal crystals, it occurs in leaf-like masses and radiating aggregates. It is an easy mineral to recognize and soapy to the touch. Graphite is found associated with metamorphic rocks in many parts of the world, including Britain. It has long been used in lubricants, for pencils and blacklead, but it cannot be regarded as a very attractive mineral.

SULPHIDES

Although some 80 or more sulphide minerals are known, we need only consider those of iron, copper, lead and zinc as common ones. The rest are rare types found in veins. As a group, they are not very long-lasting; water and air may soon destroy most sulphide minerals, which seems a pity because some of them are very beautiful.

CHALCOCITE is the simple copper sulphide, Cu_2S, and it is one of the less attractive copper minerals. It is dull grey-black to black, somewhat brittle, soft and heavy, with little flat pseudo-hexagonal prisms in clustered jumbled masses. This mineral soon oxidizes after it is removed from the ground and it is nowhere very common. The best crystals used to come from Cornwall, especially the Camborne-Redruth area, where they were about 1 cm (·5 in) in size, normally standing on edge.

BORNITE is a more common sulphide and is a 'double' sulphide species with a formula Cu_5FeS_4. It may occur in rough cubes and dodecahedra, but often it is massive. Characteristic of bornite is the way the coppery-orange fresh surfaces tarnishes to brown and intense purplish hues. This gives it its other name, 'peacock ore'. It is not very

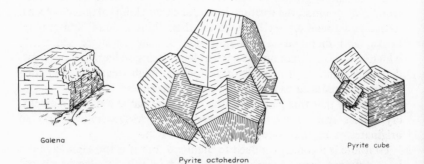

Galena

Pyrite octohedron

Pyrite cube

Metallic sulphides in the cubic system. Each has a bright metallic lustre. Galena is silvery but pyrite with its yellowish colour has earned the title 'fool's gold'.

PLATE 3. Native elements are rarely found: shown here are *above left*, bronze or greenish-stained granular or jagged copper; *right*, yellow crystalline sulphur; *below left*, thread or sliver-like silver; *right*, steely grey graphite.

PLATE 4. Some of the many forms of quartz: *top left*, cut and polished agate nodule; *right*, a broken flint nodule showing the characteristic conchoidal fracture marks; *below right*, the pyramidal end of a prism of crystalline quartz with its characteristic striations; *left*, a hollow nodule or geode with stubby crystals of (blue) amethyst. All about natural size.

hard (3) and it is of course heavy. Once again, Cornwall is the best known home of this mineral in Britain.

GALENA is one of the most famous and easily recognized of all sulphide ores because it crystallizes into beautiful cubic crystals and breaks along perfect cleavage planes parallel to the cube faces. Rare octahedra or modifications of cubes do occur. It has a splendid silver-grey colour and metallic lustre and has a lead-grey streak. Galena is the simple sulphide of lead, PbS, and it melts at a low temperature to give off fumes of evil-smelling sulphur dioxide. What is left is lead and some-times this contains a little silver.

This ore can be found in many places all over the world. Some have huge deposits and the individual crystals may be up to two inches across. Many places in Europe have mineralization with galena, and in Britain the more famous areas where it has been mined are the Truro-Liskeard district of Cornwall, the Mendip Hills, Dyfed, the Peak District, Alston Moor and Weardale, and Wanlockhead in Dumfries and Galloway.

SPHALERITE is another 'double' sulphide, formula (ZnFe)S, and it may contain up to 26% iron. Commonly it forms in tetrahedras but with slightly curved faces, brownish or black in colour and with a distinctive resinous lustre. It is not a particularly heavy or hard mineral (Mohs' scale 3–4). This zinc-iron ore is most commonly found with galena and all the galena occurrences seem to have it. Famous mining areas for sphalerite include Czechoslovakia, Germany, Romania and Spain, and in Britain especially well-known places are Cumbria, Durham, Derbyshire and Cornwall.

CHALCOPYRITE has the formula $CuFeS_2$ and is perhaps the most abundant copper mineral of all. Its crystals are rather tetrahedron shaped but large ones are very irregular. Most characteristic of chal-copyrite is its bright brassy-yellow colour when fresh, and the irri-descent tarnish it soon acquires on exposure. It has an uneven to conchoidal fracture and a poor cleavage. Chalcopyrite can be confused with pyrite, the iron sulphide, but it has a more intense colour and irridescent lustre.

Chalcopyrite is probably formed at the same temperatures as other sulphide ores, especially pyrite, so it usually accompanies them. It is known in many parts of France, Germany, Italy and other countries in Europe, and in Britain is found especially in Cornwall, Cumbria and at Wanlockhead, Scotland.

R.   D

PYRITE is the mineralogical name for 'fools' gold' because although it has a yellow brassy lustre or golden appearance, it is an iron sulphide, FeS_2. Its name is Greek in origin, referring to the sparks pyrite may produce when struck. Cubes of all sizes are common, but special forms, pyritohedra, octahedra and others, are known. They occur in cavities and veins and scattered throughout rocks in clusters and single crystals alike. The crystal faces have a distinctive striation and the mineral is heavier and harder than most other sulphides.

Of all sulphides perhaps this is the most common, abundant and fascinating. While it can be formed in veins associated with volcanic or igneous rocks, it is also present in coal and other sedimentary formations. Pyrite may replace the original skeletal stuff of fossils, and 'brass ammonites' and snail shells preserved in pyrite are in many a collector's possession. How it manages to crystallize in some of these rocks and replace so delicately all the details of the original shell is something of a puzzle.

MARCASITE is another iron sulphide, FeS_2, but although it may be chemically identical to pyrite, it is mineralogically quite distinct. It crystallizes in the orthorhombic system in rare tabular or compressed forms, but more probably it is found in aggregates of needle-like crystals making up nodules, balls and discs of radiating structure. This mineral has a pale, brassy-yellow colour, somewhat greenish in many instances, and the lustre is not so good as that of pyrite.

Marcasite occurs most commonly in rocks that have never been very hot. Sedimentary rocks such as chalk may have bands of marcasite nodules, and the mineral is also found in many of the sticky clays of southern and eastern Britain. Marcasite is a difficult mineral to preserve because it soon becomes dingy and begins to grow white 'whiskers' of iron sulphate by reaction with moist air. It needs careful washing and varnishing if it is to be kept in a collection.

OXIDES AND HYDROXIDES

While this is another large group of minerals (we could list about 150 kinds), only a very few are common and important. They occur in a variety of ways. Some form deep in veins from igneous rocks and others occur more abundantly as decomposition products from the weathering of other minerals. The sulphides can give rise to many of these oxides, but the attraction of oxygen atoms for metal atoms is so strong that oxides are resistant to further chemical attack. Because of this, most residual minerals are oxides.

CUPRITE is the copper oxide Cu_2O, and it forms in very small cubic crystals of a brownish red or purplish red colour. It has a submetallic lustre, is moderately hard (4) and very heavy. On heating it gives metallic copper and is often found with native copper. Cuprite occurs in most of the areas already mentioned above, and it is particularly well known from mines near Redruth and Liskeard, Cornwall.

Magnetite   Haematite

Magnetite occurs as tiny black pyramids and haematite is called 'kidney ore' because of its rounded shapes.

HAEMATITE has a name to remind us of the blood-red colour of its powder, and is iron oxide, Fe_2O_3. Sometimes it is called 'kidney ore' because it occurs in globose red-brown masses looking like kidneys. It also has a mica-like form where it occurs as tiny, steely grey flakes with a brilliant metallic lustre. Haematite belongs to the hexagonal system, but this is not obvious in many of the compact or globose forms. It is a brittle mineral, heavy and hard (6.5) and it gives a deep red streak. This iron ore occurs very widely indeed and is found in almost ever kind of rock, igneous, volcanic, metamorphic and sedimentary, in veins, beds and cavities, and it may even replace the original material of fossils. Famous mines for haematite occur in Devon, Cornwall, South Wales, Cumbria and Lancashire.

CASSITERITE is not a common mineral but it is an interesting oxide of tin, SnO_2, found in Cornwall and in a few other parts of the world. It is our most important source of tin. It occurs in stubby prisms or pyramids of the tetragonal system, but it is difficult to make out which faces are which. Cassiterite crystals are normally shiny to dull, sharp-edged and black, but the mineral also occurs as granular and cauliflower-like granules. It is hard and very heavy. Many of the Cornish mines yielded great quantities of vein cassiterite in the past and there may be other deposits still to be found in that part of the country. 'Placer' tinstone – grains and fragments of cassiterite washed from the veins on the granite and slate uplands – have been dug and panned from the gravels of most of the Cornish rivers.

GOETHITE is the hydroxide of iron, $Fe_2O_3 \cdot H_2O$, and it usually occurs in a non-crystalline form, massive or encrusting rock surfaces. This form has the old name *limonite*. It is an earthy, usually soft, yellow-brown, red or even black substance, but rare, hard (5.5) orthorhombic crystals may also occur. Virtually every other known iron mineral will 'rust' and decompose into goethite and it is easily transported as tiny particles by water. This helps make it one of the most abundant and widespread of all colouring matters in rocks. Many of the colours ranging from yellow and red to black in sedimentary rocks of all kinds are due to goethite. It also coats and lines cavities, fissures and pore spaces in almost every conceivable geological situation, and in many instances it acts as the cement which binds minerals or rock fragments into a consolidated rock.

MAGNETITE was mentioned as a rock-forming mineral. It is iron oxide, Fe_3O_4, which in some of its varieties may also include magnesium, manganese, nickel or zinc. The crystals are usually very small, octahedra or dodecahedra, hard (6) and heavy, and an intense black with a metallic lustre. They are first formed at high temperatures in molten rocks and can be found in basalts and other dark igneous rocks and as small grains in granites. Instances of magnetite in veins are common, and the mineral may replace others formed earlier. It resists weathering to a considerable degree.

Nowhere in Britain has yielded much magnetite in large discrete bodies, but the deposits in Sweden are famous, and there are localities yielding good magnetite crystals in Austria and in northern Italy. As the name tells us, magnetite is a magnetic (iron) ore and also goes by the old name of lodestone. It served the navigators and travellers of old in the role of a compass.

ODDS AND ENDS

Here we look at a few important minerals that are in different chemical classes. They are usually associated with those just described and in previous times miners cast them hastily aside. Today many are important to industry and old tip heaps may be reworked to obtain them.

FLUORITE is a common and simple mineral, calcium fluoride, CaF_2. Its importance lies in its use as a flux to help smelting and refining of metals, a property known for very many centuries. Fluorite crystallizes in simple cubes for the most part; many are twinned and clustered in cavities or lining fissures. It is a brittle mineral, soft (4) and light, transparent when pure but often with attractive, though pale, colours – all the hues of the rainbow. Some such crystals have been used as gems, but they are not very brilliant.

Some of the best fluorite crystals in Europe come from Britain where they have several different origins – vein minerals and replacements of rocks attacked by hot fluorine-bearing fluids or gases. Many of the cubes are about an inch across, with the best coming from mines in Derbyshire and Cumbria. Devon and Cornwall have also yielded fluorite.

Derbyshire has its own variety called 'Blue John', which is massive, granular, deep purple-banded, blue and colourless. It has long been used as an ornamental stone and even cut into cups, vases and other large ornaments. Deposits of this stone also occur in southern Germany. Massive granular fluorite is quarried and dug on a large scale in several countries for the smelting industries.

SIDERITE, iron carbonate, $FeCO_3$, is found mostly as a brown mineral with small rhombohedral crystals, dull, soft and not very heavy. The crystals have somewhat curved faces: they look like sphalerite but are paler. To distinguish siderite we note it dissolves in hydrochloric acid, slowly when cold but rapidly when hot. The best crystals in Britain have been obtained in the Cornish mines and good deposits have long been worked in southern Germany, Austria, Italy and France, and in most of these places it seems that siderite replaces calcium carbonate in veins and cavities.

MALACHITE is leaf-green in colour and is a carbonate of copper, $Cu_2(OH)_2CO_3$. Although its crystals are fine monoclinic prisms, it invariably seems to occur as an encrusting mineral, compact and dense.

Although it is rather brittle, it has been valued since prehistoric times as an ornamental stone as well as a copper ore, since it has such an attractive range of emerald green and other green hues and is not too hard (3–4). Polished material, especially the botryoidal (or bulbous) forms, may show beautiful colour banding. Some of the most extensive deposits in Europe occur in the Ural Mountains; the Czars of Russia had a room encrusted with polished malachite in the Winter Palace at Leningrad. Only small amounts of it ever seem to have been exploited in Britain, for example in Cornwall and the Lake District.

AZURITE is the other vivid copper carbonate, $Cu_3(OH)_2(CO_3)_2$, having an intense blue. It occurs in sharp-edged lustrous crystals in a variety of shapes of the monoclinic system. It is soft (3), well cleaved, not heavy and, above all, very blue.

Many parts of the world yield azurite and it is a mineral prized by collectors for its wonderful colour. Unfortunately there are not many places in Europe which still yield it, but the areas for copper ores that we have already mentioned still occasionally provide specimens.

BARITE is barium sulphate, $BaSO_4$, one of the few sulphates found associated with vein minerals. Of all its characteristic properties, its weight is most obvious, and it has been called 'heavy spar'. Large, orthorhombic tabular, white or clear crystals are not uncommon and they have well marked cleavage and are not very hard (3). Barite forms at low temperatures in veins and cavities in all kinds of rocks. Some of the best crystals known anywhere in the world come from Britain. Cumbria, Northumberland and Derbyshire have all produced splendid material. Today the mineral is important as a source of barium for the chemical industry, as a filler for fine papers and paints and for mud used in drilling for oil.

Barite (barytes) is very easily identified by its crystal shapes – flat, blade or tablet-like.

CELESTITE is the strontium sulphate $SrSO_4$ and is not a very common mineral. It has much the same crystal form as barite but also occurs massive in cross-fibre veins and as long tablets. Similarly it is clear, transparent or white, though it may have reddish or bluish tinges which distinguish it from barite. Celestite occurs mainly in sedimentary rocks, where it lines cavities and fills fissures. There are deposits in North America, Germany and other parts of Europe, but among the best are those from around Yate and Bristol in England, where the crystals reach many inches in size and occur in a soft red clay formation.

APATITE is a rather complicated mineral composed of several elements, but basically it is a calcium phosphate, $Ca_5(F, Cl, OH)(PO_4)_3$. It occurs in many forms and in many rocks. The crystals are commonly hexagonal prisms with pyramidal ends, or tabular hexagonal forms. In colour it may be apple-green, yellow or brown; many specimens have an oily appearance or a vitreous or resinous lustre. It rates hardness 5 in Mohs' scale. The best crystals occur in pegmatites associated with granitic rocks in may parts of North and South America, Scandinavia and Czechoslovakia. There seems never to have been much found in Britain.

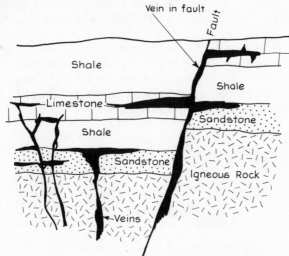

Mineral veins, (shown in black) are usually introduced into an area from some sort of igneous parent body. They may merely form along planes of weakness and in cavities in the rocks or they may actually replace masses of rock previously there.

HOW METALLIC ORES OCCUR

A visitor to almost any mining area where metallic ores are produced will soon discover that the miners find not one but several different minerals together. Perhaps more than one is useful, and the miners take great care to separate and keep them. They throw away the minerals they don't need, and these they usually call 'gangue' minerals. Certain ores and gangue minerals always occur together and are found in the same kinds of rock. Over the centuries miners and geologists have come to recognize where large deposits of metallic ores are to be found.

The mining geologist recognizes three kinds of ore deposits:

1. those formed by igneous activity;
2. those formed by weathering and other processes produced by running water;
3. those formed by metamorphism.

There are several types of deposits in each of these categories. Let us deal first with those in the igneous group. They were among the earliest ore deposits ever to be formed when the earth's crust began to solidify many millions of years ago. The other categories came later.

Magmatic deposits are formed in igneous rocks when they crystallize or solidify from molten rock or magma. The ore is scattered throughout the igneous rock or perhaps gathered into clumps and masses near its margins. Nickel, chromium and similar metals are found in ores of this kind, as are diamonds and corundum.

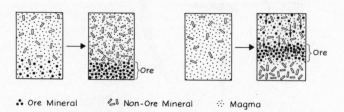

∴ Ore Mineral   ⌀ Non-Ore Mineral   ∵ Magma

Ore deposition from a magma. On the left, the heavier metallic ore minerals crystallize at an early stage and sink to the bottom of the magma body. On the right, the ore minerals crystallize rather late and settle into a layer high up. (After L. F. Laporte).

Pegmatitic deposits are formed at the end of the magmatic or rock-forming stage. In these the minerals occur in small masses and dykes near the edge of the igneous rock body. For the most part they were produced at rather low temperatures. Pegmatite veins seem to have cooled slowly, so the crystals are often of large size and beautifully shaped. The best feldspar, mica and quartz minerals occur in this way.

Hydrothermal deposits, the name tells us, were formed from hot fluids. The minerals were deposited in cracks, fissures and cavities in the igneous and surrounding rocks after the consolidation of the hot igneous mass. There is an enormous range of metallic ores to be found in these deposits. Most of the ores we have described on previous pages occur this way. Some were crystallized at high temperature while others did not form till most of the heat had been lost.

Pneumatolytic deposits may be produced at the last gasp of the igneous activity or at some rather earlier stage. They are remarkable in that they seem to result from the activity of hot vapours and gas. This may attack minerals recently formed in the igneous rock, the surrounding formations, and the new mineral veins or lodes. Generally they are associated with granite-like rocks and pegmatites. Quite a few minerals in Cornwall originated in this way.

Among the deposits formed by surface agencies – weathering, erosion and deposition – we have *placer* or *alluvial* deposits. Many of the old gold miners panned gold from river sands and gravels of this kind. The heavy and resistant ore accumulated along the stream valleys and beaches as it was washed down from veins in the hills. Panning or modern placer mining relies merely on washing away all the light mud and sand to leave the gold, or diamonds, or cassiterite or other minerals behind.

Residual deposits occur when the original minerals have been deeply weathered and much of their bulk has been removed by weathering. Here sheets or pockets of ore may remain – the mineral remnants of previous rock bodies. Some of these deposits may, in fact, overlie *enriched* deposits because water carrying minerals in solution has percolated down into the ground and left new minerals there.

Metamorphic rocks have been subjected to change and this comes about by pressure or heat, or both. When metamorphism occurs because of

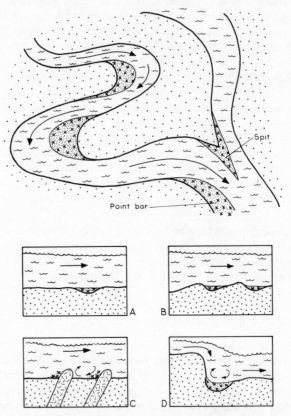

Placer deposits accumulate in streams draining mineral-rich land. They occur where slack water or some obstruction holds back the movement of the heavier (ore) particles but still washes away the clay sand or soil fragments. A, A simple hollow in the stream bed. B, Depressions between ripple marks or sand banks. C, Concentration behind a reef or resistant crag. D, The hollow at the foot of a waterfall or rapids.

the upsurging of a magma body in the crust it is a result of the great heat and pressure. The local effects near the edge of the igneous rock we call *contact metamorphism*. Accompanying the heat and pressure there is usually a lot of vapour and gas which attacks the rock. From this onslaught new minerals may result, and are called *metasomatic* or

Many metallic minerals occur in fairly well-marked zones around parent granite intrusions. Those crystallizing at the highest temperatures are confined near the granite but others such as lead or iron can escape to a greater distance before solidifying.

replacement minerals. Many tin, copper, iron and other metallic ores are formed in this way.

Sedimentary ores (of iron, copper, lead or zinc) are those in which the original bedded rock has somehow been replaced by metallic oxides, sulphides, carbonates or silicates. They may not be very rich but they do occur locally in enormous quantities.

What, then, in any particular region determines which kind of ores will be formed and where? We do not know all the answers even in the most intensely studied areas, but geologists believe that ore is where it is because of certain interacting geological factors. Igneous rocks occur in areas where the crust of the earth has been in movement and where once deeply buried parts are now exposed, and where volcanic activity breaks out or once did so. Zones of weakness in the crust allow magma to escape from the great pressures below, and the magma brings minerals. At the surface erosion, especially by water, may alter, redistribute and concentrate minerals in various ways. Rivers carry away sediment to the sea, but not all of it may be lost; there is now a new search for submarine mineral deposits. We need minerals from the sea floor and from the rocks under the sea-bed. In the next century man will surely extend his mining activities below the realm of the fishes.

CHAPTER 4

VULCAN'S FORGE: THE IGNEOUS ROCKS

MANY of the rocks at the surface of the earth are obviously composed of crystals. Some have big crystals, others are made exclusively of crystals only just visible to the naked eye. These bodies of rock are of different shapes, compositions, sizes and ages. In many of them one can easily see the rock-forming minerals are few in number. In others the crystals are too small to identify, or even too small to see. We call these respectively coarse-grained, medium-grained and fine-grained rocks. On rare occasions one may come across volcanic rocks, solidified lava, that are just like glass. At first sight there may not be much to relate these different kinds of rocks to one another, but under the microscope their similarities may become clear.

Some of the early geologists thought that all the crystalline rocks had been precipitated from an evaporating ocean far back in the history of the earth. However, when it was found that volcanoes erupt molten lava which may contain the familiar rock-forming crystals and that some old volcanic rocks consist very largely of such crystals, this theory began to crumble. It was then not long before geologists were claiming that most of the crystalline rocks, including granites and basalts, were not precipitates but were solidified from once molten matter, like lava. Tremendous heat seems to be needed to melt rock so the term *igneous* (fire-formed) rocks was invented. As mentioned on p. 33, igneous rocks are solidified from molten rock material called *magma*.

We think that igneous rocks formed the first crust of the earth, long before it was cool enough for the atmosphere and seas to exist as they do today. In the millions of years that have passed since then, all other rocks have been derived from those first igneous formations. From time to time new molten rock seeps or bursts out at the surface in *volcanic* eruptions. Some molten rock fails to reach the surface but is kept below by the strength of the formations of rock above. It may remain trapped to solidify as an igneous *intrusion*. Just what happens to magma as it seeks to escape upwards from the great pressures and heat within the crust very largely controls the characteristics of the resulting igneous rock. A diagram can show best the shapes that a body of igneous material may acquire.

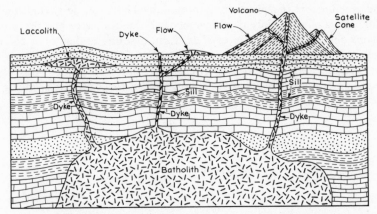

Igneous rocks enter the outer layers of the crust from below in a variety of shapes and sizes. Where they do not reach the surface they remain as *intrusions*; at the surface they are *extrusive* and produce lava flows and volcanoes.

It is in volcanoes that we see igneous rocks in the making, and it is from them that we have gained many of our ideas. There are different kinds of volcanic eruptions and different shapes of volcanoes. To a large degree these kinds are dependent upon the nature of the upswelling magma. Magma itself is a complex material – a sort of 'witches brew' of molten rock material, very hot and under great pressure. Apart from the elements that make up the minerals, magma has other ingredients – water vapour and gases. When escaping magma nears the surface the water vapour comes to the top like bubbles in soda-water. Here it may accumulate until there is enough pressure to burst through the overlying cover as a volcanic explosion. Magma that contains lots of hot gas and water vapour tends to be fluid, but as these volatiles escape it becomes sluggish and stiff. Truly vast quantities of steam and gases are given off every time a volcano erupts, and long after the eruption of lava or solid ash is over, steam and gas continue to rise from the depths.

VOLCANIC ROCKS

Flowing or bursting out at the surface, magma produces several kinds of material – solid, blown out by explosions or a blast of gas, liquid known as *lava*, and gas. In the cold air lava soon cools into solid rock. If it is very rapidly chilled it congeals into a natural *glass* with no individual rock-forming mineral crystals at all. The silica tetrahedra and metallic ions in a glass are all intermingled in a disorderly confused mass. In cooling rapidly they have not had the chance to link up into chains and sheets and form crystals. Lava erupting under water congeals into pillow-shaped masses, each with a chilled crust and a more granular interior. This is a feature called pillow-lava, and it can be found among some of the world's most ancient rocks as well as among some of the most recently formed.

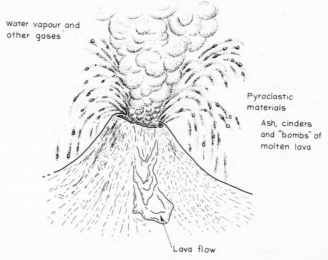

Water vapour and other gases

Pyroclastic materials

Ash, cinders and "bombs" of molten lava

Lava flow

Volcanoes are where the hot gases and solid or molten rock from within the crust burst out: they are among the most important and spectacular means earth has of releasing its internal energy.

Volcanic explosions break up and scatter the solidified lava. This debris may eventually become consolidated into *pyroclastic* rocks (those 'broken by fire'). This stuff ranges from fine dust to chunks the size of houses. We speak of volcanic ash, blocks, bombs – rounded masses of congealing magma shot through the air – and cinders. Most of it looks burnt and cindery. *Pumice* is a volcanic froth – a rock in which the gases were trapped as bubbles, giving a honeycombed type of structure, light enough to float.

Volcanic ash falls upon the land surface or into the sea to produce layers that soon harden into rock. To these the name *tuff* is given where the ash particles are small: rocks made from large angular fragments are called *agglomerates* or *volcanic breccias*.

Volcanic bombs

Pillow lava

Volcanic rocks take on many shapes as they are extruded and cooled. Blocks of molten lava shot through the air by an explosion of gases may acquire strange fruit-like or bomb-like forms. Erupting into water, basaltic lava solidifies into pillow like masses. Gas and steam hollows (vesicles) may become filled with minerals.

Ancient volcanic rocks form wide areas of the hills and uplands of North Wales, the English Lakeland and parts of Scotland. They crop out in numerous places in South-west Wales, Devon and Cornwall, Charnwood Forest and the Cheviots. And in the Inner Hebrides and Northern Ireland are relics of a great volcanic province with volcanic rocks, basalt floods, ashes, and many kinds of igneous intrusions. During the Cainozoic era this part of western Europe must have echoed to many an eruption, and several thousand square miles of land were added to the continent by the piling up of ash and lava.

THE FORMATION OF IGNEOUS ROCKS

Apart from the rapidly chilled and solidified rock glasses, each igneous rock is made up of a distinctive assemblage of minerals. All the constituents necessary to form igneous rocks are present in magmas. Another word sometimes used instead of magma is *melt,* and in a melt the ions are all highly agitated, that is, at a high temperature. As the magma loses energy and cools, the different ions within it link up into various assemblages, mostly of silicates, but also of oxides and sulphides as the temperature continues to drop. These new collections of ions grow in regular fashion, as described in Chapter 2, and the process of *crystallization* is under way. The liquid melt becomes clouded with the beginnings of crystals which grow until the melt is all used up and a solid crystalline mass is formed. At various stages in the lowering of the temperature of the melt different combinations of ions are possible and the rock-forming minerals are produced.

Lava flows and bombs, volcanic ashes and agglomerates add new material to the surface of the earth. Volcanic gases contribute to the atmosphere and hydrosphere. But what of the magma below the surface? Denied escape above, it slowly cools and solidifies into solid igneous rock, affecting the rocks around and above it and perhaps bringing masses of new or important mineral deposits with it.

The rock-forming minerals always crystallize in a definite order. To a large extent the mineralogical composition of an igneous rock depends upon the manner and order in which the crystallization of the silicates takes place. Several things influence this. In most magmas there are the ingredients both for the ferromagnesian minerals and for the non-ferromagnesian rock-forming minerals. The kinds and amounts of these that are precipitated by the time the melt is used up or solidified control not only the composition of the rock but also the relationships between the crystals themselves.

Interruptions in crystallization can occur, as when the gases in a magma escape and the fluid part then becomes sluggish and viscous. In other cases early-formed crystals may sink or be otherwise removed so that only a part of the magma is represented by them. Rapidly cooled magma has little chance to develop large crystals, but in the slowly cooled material crystals may be not only large but also perfectly formed. Rate of crystallization depends in large measure upon depth – the deeper, the slower as a rule.

For some reason a magma may cool at variable rates, perhaps slowly at first, then more rapidly. The first-formed crystals may already be large when the cooling rate quickens. Between the large crystals, or *phenocrysts,* the remaining melt quickly produces countless tiny crystals in what appears to be an attempt to get all its ions into crystals before the temperature drops too much. The result is called a *porphyry,* a rock containing phenocrysts set in a fine-grained ground mass. Some rare porphyries have their phenocrysts embedded in a glassy chilled groundmass. Here the magma was perhaps erupted as lava at the surface after the large crystals had formed.

In some igneous rocks two different species of minerals crystallize at the same time and penetrate each other. This intergrowth may be on a large scale, as it commonly is with some kinds of feldspar, or it may be so fine as to be called *micrographic.* Olivine is a mineral which seems to form early in the crystallization of a melt, and the olivine crystals in some cases may be enclosed by a later crystallizing pyroxene mineral. We call this a *poikilitic* texture. Where feldspars are found intergrown with augite the term *ophitic* is used. In other circumstances a cooling igneous melt may develop cavities in which the later-forming

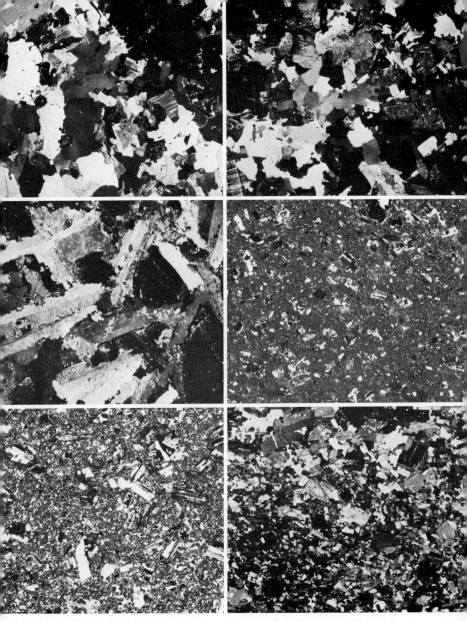

PLATE 5. Transparent slices of acidic and intermediate igneous rocks seen
under the microscope and using a polarised light source to emphasise the
different crystal constituents. *Top left and right*, granite (white quartz, grey
feldspar and dark mica). *Centre left*, syenite, a coarse-grained sodium-rich
rock from Norway. *Right*, hornblende andesite, an intermediate fine-
grained type from Germany. *Below left*, trachyte, another fine-grained
and porphyritic intermediate rock from Germany. *Right*, quartz mica
diorite, a coarser-grained acidic type from Germany. Magnifications
approx. ×35.

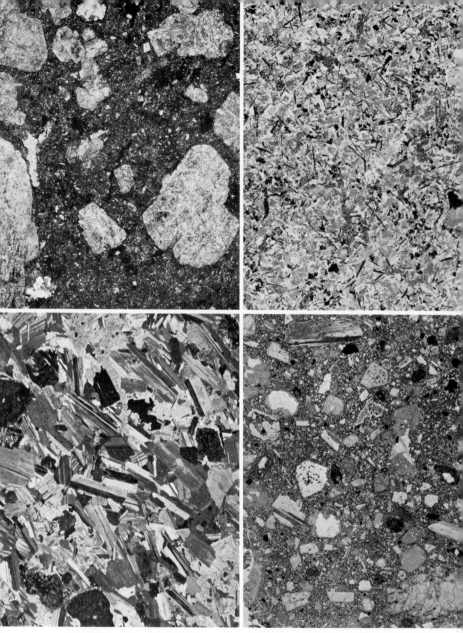

PLATE 6. Transparent slices of basic igneous rocks. *Above left*, porphyritic basalt, from Cumbria, with large phenocrysts of feldspar. *Right*, dolerite, a fine-grained basic rock from Edinburgh, with plagioclase feldspar, augite and olivine. *Below left*, coarse-grained olivine gabbro from Scotland shows large laths of plagioclase feldspar and darker crystals of augite and olivine. *Right*, olivine basalt, Edinburgh, with phenocrysts of feldspar and of olivine. Magnifications approx. ×35.

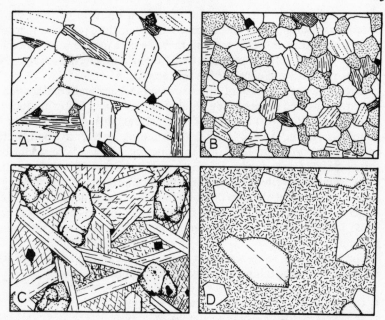

Textures in igneous rocks. A, Granitic texture, many crystals have (true) natural boundaries developed. B, Granular or sugary texture in which the crystals are all of the same size but true crystal boundaries are not present. C, Ophitic texture in which large augite crystals enclose laths of plagioclase feldspar. D, Porphyritic texture involves large crystals or *phenocrysts* embedded in a finer crystalline matrix. All are magnified approximately 20 times.

crystals can form. The crystals in these *drusy cavities* have commonly been able to grow unimpeded by a crush of other crystals around them. They may thus be more or less perfect crystal forms.

TYPES OF IGNEOUS ROCKS

With so many different factors and conditions to affect the final composition and texture of an igneous rock it is no wonder that there are so many varieties. The business of classifying them all has been worrying geologists for years, and many classifications and 'family trees' of igneous rocks have been produced. All these are of course for our convenience, and all rely to some extent upon characteristics that

R.   E the geologist cannot determine for himself in the field or from hand specimens. Composition and texture have been the properties that we have looked at in this chapter, and they are perhaps the most suitable for the majority of geologists to use. Colour and specific gravity are further properties to consider in this connection.

The immense numbers of different compositions and combinations of textures has led to a daunting number of rock names being produced. Most names are coined from those of the places where the rock occur – andesite from the Andes, larvikite from Larvik in Norway, borolanite from Loch Borolan in Scotland, to name but a few. There would be little point in remembering even half of them. Generally speaking, the most important criteria to use are the proportions of the different rock-forming minerals present. With lots of ferromagnesian (or mafic) minerals present, the rock is dark in colour and said to be *melanocratic*, while *leucocratic* rocks are pale and contain less than 30% of mafic minerals.

For simplicity's sake, we might group all the known igneous rocks into four sets depending upon their composition:

1. 60% to 100% light minerals – granitic and rhyolitic rocks.
2. 30% to 60% light minerals – intermediate rocks.
3. less than 30% light minerals – basaltic and gabbroic rocks.
4. less than 25% light minerals – ultrabasic rocks.

The last set is a rather rare and special category but the first three can be fitted into a diagram (opposite) which shows the proportion of silicates in each of the major families of igneous rocks that we will recognize in this book.

As one can see, the graph shows the percentages of rock-forming minerals in the composition and gives the idea that there is a continuous progression from rocks in which light-coloured minerals predominate to those in which the melanocratic minerals are commonest. The names of the rocks are rather arbitrarily fixed on the basis of the composition and the texture. As we move on the chart from rocks of a light colour to rocks of a darker colour we consider those with a higher content of ferromagnesian minerals. Generally speaking, the darker the colour the higher the specific gravity of the rock. Colour and specific gravity, together with texture and recognizable mineral content, offer ready means of describing and classifying the igneous rocks. Composition is, of course, a fundamental property; texture may well relate to depth of burial on cooling (i.e. time taken for the magma to crystallize). It is easier by far to estimate the composition of a rock when one can see and identify all the crystals or grains within it. The finer-grained igneous rocks are more difficult to name. Porphyries offer us phenocrysts by which to name them, but the matrix is also important and may be difficult to analyse without a microscope.

Perhaps at this point we should take a moment to mention how rocks are examined under the microscope. A thin flat slice of the material is firmly fixed by a transparent cement to a glass slide. It is afterwards ground on carborundum powders on a glass plate or buff until it is thin enough to be transparent (about 0.03 mm thick). At this thickness it can be examined so that the optical properties of each of the minerals present are found and the minerals identified and their relationships to one another seen. Under the microscope the mineral composition of most of the fine-grained rocks may thus be recognized relatively easily.

The diagram also shows how the proportions of silica and feldspars,

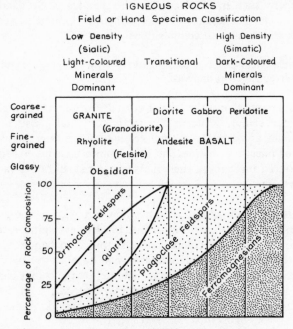

A table to show the composition of different kinds of igneous rock. Only a few of the very many rock names used are shown here.

and the kinds of feldspars, are important in our classification scheme. With relatively high proportions of quartz, feldspars rich in potassium are common, but as the proportion of quartz diminishes so the feldspars with sodium and calcium, i.e. the plagioclase feldspars, increase in importance. Generally speaking, the higher the proportion of ferro-magnesian minerals, the higher is the proportion of calcium to be found in the plagioclase feldspars. Expressed another way, the most 'basic' igneous rocks have the highest proportions of plagioclase feldspar, and especially the calcium feldspar, while the most 'acid' igneous rocks have 65% or more of quartz together with orthoclase feldspars.

Granitic rocks

Granites and *granodiorites* are said to comprise about 95% of all the intrusive igneous rocks in the outermost 15 km (9-10 miles) of the crust. Most of them occur as large – even gigantic – intrusions, batholiths, associated with the Precambrian shields or with old mountain areas. There are many such in Scotland, and the granites of Scotland, the Lake District, Devon and Cornwall are batholiths. Granite is a coarse-grained rock with a mineral composition:

2 parts orthoclase feldspar + 1 part quartz + 1 part plagioclase and small amounts of ferromagnesian minerals

The feldspars may form the largest crystals in the rock, white, pink or yellowish in colour, while the quartz is clear and glassy and the ferromagnesians are dark. Some granites have more than one variety of feldspar or mica, tourmaline, and other minor constituents such as zircon. Scattered throughout their mass may be small rare crystals of metallic ores.

Rhyolites are rocks of granitic composition but with a fine-grained texture. Fresh rhyolite is grey, white, buff, black or even pink in colour, and in many rhyolites the colours are distributed in bands. Since it was once a thick and viscous kind of lava, rhyolite tends to have curved and contorted flow lines, and these are marked by the colour changes. Gas holes or vesicles are common and may be lined with crystals. *Pumice* is commonly a rhyolitic lava froth, but basaltic pumices are known.

Many fine-grained intrusive rhyolites have phenocrysts of quartz and feldspar which must have been brought up from the depths below. A few such rocks are rather like nougat containing pieces of nut or candied fruit. Quartz phenocrysts in the rhyolite lead us to call it a *quartz porphyry*, but quartz and feldspar phenocrysts together gives a rock called a *rhyolite porphyry*.

Obsidian is a natural glass which, despite its dark appearance, may have a composition like granite.

Pitchstone is the name for another dark and glassy rock which, like obsidian, has a glass-sharp edge and a conchoidal fracture when broken. Pitchstone has a granitic chemical composition. Both of these glassy rocks occur as old lava flows and as small intrusions. The colour of a natural glass is not a reliable guide to its composition and it is virtually impossible in hand specimens to tell the difference between granitic and basaltic varieties.

Basaltic and gabbroic rocks

It is a fairly safe bet that almost any common dark igneous rock belongs to the basalt-gabbro group. Well over 90% of the total lava flows known are of this kind of material. They are heavy tough rocks, rich in ferromagnesian minerals.

Basalt is a fine-grained igneous rock, composed of approximately:

    1 part plagioclase feldspars
    1 part ferromagnesian minerals (usually augite and olivine)

The feldspars take the form of tiny lath-shaped crystals in most fine- and medium-grained basalts, while the ferromagnesian minerals are mostly stubby prisms or tablets; some may be intergrown with each other. Many a basalt has a liberal sprinkling of minute magnetite and pyrite cubes throughout its mass. In some the olivine is badly decomposed into other greenish minerals.

Most basalts are dense rocks, with a faintly granular texture. Some have small phenocrysts of olivine or pyroxene: one or two have hornblende crystals.

Gabbro is the coarse-grained variety. *Peridotite* is the name for the olivine-rich variety with little plagioclase feldspar, peridot being another word for olivine.

Other names for these rocks are *diabase* and *dolerite* and they are defined by some geologists as intermediate in grain-size between basalts and gabbros.

Being richer in iron compounds than the granitic rocks, the basalts and gabbros weather more readily. Oxidation and hydration of the ferromagnesian minerals changes them from blue, green, black or grey colours when fresh to rusty yellows, red and browns. Perhaps the basalts of the Isle of Skye and Antrim, Northern Ireland, and at Edinburgh are the most famous in Britain. They give rise to unusual beauty spots such as Fingal's Cave and the Giant's Causeway.

Intermediate igneous rocks

There really is no sharp break in composition between the two sets of rocks we have just described – they blend continuously from one to the other. Between the two edges of our chart, squarely in the middle however, are the andesites and diorites.

Andesite is the term for the fine-grained igneous rocks intermediate between rhyolite and basalt in composition. They were first identified from volcanoes in the Andes mountains of South America, and have since been recognized in very many other places. Under the hand lens most of these rocks are rather granular in appearance.

Diorites are coarser-grained varieties, generally pale in colour. The dark minerals they contain are pyroxenes and hornblende rather than biotite. Some intermediate rocks, while still below the surface, have been altered by hot gases and water vapour. These have broken down the original iron-bearing silicates to give the rocks rather handsome and locally mottled deep green colours.

Alkali rocks

These are rare igneous intrusive rocks which contain much sodium plagioclase feldspar and other sodium minerals. We think the magma from which they solidified had in many cases become contaminated with calcium carbonate from limestone which was 'dissolved' by the hot fluid. The calcium combined with the silica in the magma to form slightly heavier new minerals which then sank, leaving a sodium-rich liquid behind. When this remaining liquid crystallized it produced the sodium-plagioclase feldspar in abundance.

'Left-overs'

When the rock-forming minerals have crystallized from the magma there may still be a lot of water vapour and gases trapped within the mush of crystals. These gassy left-overs may contain a wide variety of metallic and other elements. Some, such as fluorine and boron, are quite capable of attacking the feldspar crystals. Others await the lowering of temperature that allows them to solidify into crystals of metallic ores or new silicates. The granites of South-west England were bedevilled by such 'left-overs' after they had largely crystallized, which is the prime reason why so many valued mineral deposits are associated with them.

IGNEOUS ROCKS, RADIOACTIVITY AND GEOLOGICAL TIME

All that we know about igneous rocks suggests that deep in the earth the temperatures are very high and that they have been this way for a very long time indeed. One of the sources of heat may be in radioactivity, the process by which the nuclei of some elements spontaneously throw off particles. In doing so they generate energy and produce new elements. Not long after the beginning of this century it was suggested that the process of radioactivity might be measured and used to discover how old the radioactive minerals are. The idea has been a productive one and has led to the development of analytical techniques which seem to yield reasonably trustworthy data whereby to measure the ages of many different, but principally igneous, kinds of rocks.

If we know what new elements result from the process of radioactive decay of a parent element and the rate at which the decay takes place we have in effect a sort of geological clock. We can illustrate the idea by referring to a rather vigorously radioactive element, uranium – 238, $_{92}U238$. Its decomposition end-products are the gas helium, and lead $_{82}Pb^{206}$. The rate at which this decomposition takes place is known and seems to be constant and unaffected by other changes. This rate is known as the *half-life* of the element – the time needed for half of the nuclei in the sample of that element to decay. The half-life of uranium 238 is 4.56×10^9 – or 4560 million years. The ratio of lead −206 to uranium 238 in any sample depends on how long the process of decay has been going on. Presumably the decay began the moment the radioactive mineral was formed. To determine its age we need to measure the ratio of lead to uranium in the mineral.

Now this assumes that the rate of decay has been constant, and from various sources we have evidence that suggests it is. The radioactive decay shown by uranium-238 is shown by other elements also present in minerals. If these minerals were formed at the same time as the rock in which they are enclosed they will indicate the age of the rock itself.

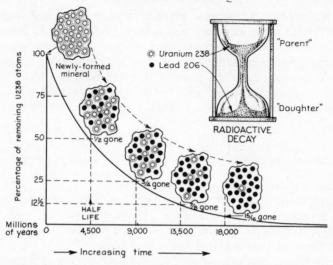

Radio-active time-piece, uranium 238 changes to lead 206. The curved line traces the slow break-down of the parent uranium over thousands of millions of years. As time goes by more and more atoms of U238 disintegrate to leave lead 206. (After Fagan).

Of course the analysis of these rocks and minerals is a very delicate, complex and lengthy business, but it has been carried out on thousands of specimens from all over the world. Most of these rocks are igneous rocks and the dates are based not just upon an analysis of selected identifiable radioactive minerals but upon the entire composition of the rock.

The decay of several other radioactive elements can be measured in this way and they all confirm that geological time is immense. Even the most careful analyses suggest that we should regard the ages indicated as rather close approximations and not very accurate determinations. The older the sample the greater may be the loss of end products which we cannot measure. The youngest minerals for which the method can be used are about two million years old. Only the decay of the radioactive isotope of carbon, carbon-14, can be used to measure very short periods of time, 50,000 years or less, and geologically that is not long.

CHAPTER 5

THE MIXING POT:
SEDIMENTARY ROCKS

In many cities of the world the old buildings and monuments are in need of repair. The stonework has decayed and the faces on the statues are no longer recognizable; on the older tombstones names are hard to read. For this destruction we blame the frost, rain, sun and wind, and the atmosphere, and the process is called *weathering*. It is the result of changes that take place in the minerals and rock in contact with the atmosphere, water and plant and animal life.

Only when part of the old building falls down do the effects of weathering come violently to our notice, but the weathering processes go quietly on all the time. They are an essential part of geology, providing new kinds of material for new kinds of rocks. The debris and products of weathering may come to rest locally as sediment, perhaps in a gutter or drain, eventually in rivers, lakes and the sea. From such sediments sedimentary rocks are born.

Weathering is then the first step in the long series of events which leads to the formation of sedimentary rocks. It takes place in two ways – mechanical and chemical. Mechanical weathering breaks down rock into smaller and smaller fragments, doing so by physical energy. Warming by the sun, cooling and splitting by frost, the action of running water, wind or ice, and the activities of living things all disrupt the rocks and their mantle of debris, the soil, above them. In the soil especially there is a constant mixing and churning activity by worms, ants, moles and other creatures.

Chemical weathering usually goes on at the same time and is a much more complex process. While mechanical weathering does not alter the rock composition, chemical weathering does.

Most essential for chemical processes is a supply of water. Not only will water dissolve a few minerals or react with them, but it may contain dissolved gases. Most commonly these are carbon dioxide or sulphur dioxide, which with the water form acids that attack many minerals. Rainwater is almost invariably a very weak acid; it contains dissolved carbon dioxide. Given time, it will decompose many minerals, and it will dissolve limestone and carry away new material in solution.

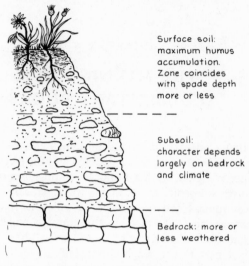

Surface soil:
maximum humus
accumulation.
Zone coincides
with spade depth
more or less

Subsoil:
character depends
largely on bedrock
and climate

Bedrock: more or
less weathered

The formation of soil.

Feldspars attacked by rainwater yield clay, soluble carbonate and
residual silica. Ferromagnesian minerals give iron oxides, soluble
carbonate, silica and clays.

Wherever there is opportunity then for air, moisture and organic
matter (often acidic) to react with minerals, changes will occur. These
weathering changes happen very largely in the uppermost few metres
of the crust of the earth which is where the necessary elements are
most common. Deeper down they become less conspicuous, much less
important. Some rocks weather rapidly; others break down only slowly.
All produce some surface debris and usually this is mixed with de-
composing vegetable matter. In this we have perhaps the most important and vital geological material of all – the soil.

There are many different kinds of soils, each depending on the
underlying kind of rock, the kinds of weathering going on, the nature
of the climate and vegetation, and so on. The subject deserves a book
to itself, but we must leave it aside here because soil is only one stage
in the story of sedimentary rocks.

The next stage in the sequence involves the removal and transport
of rock decomposition products. Wind, water, ice and organisms may
all help in this. Wind and rain carry away particles of soil and rock;
dust is blown away and heavier fragments are washed into streams

when the rains splatter down. Streams carry away a load of dissolved matter and insoluble *sediment*. Ultimately they flow into lakes or the sea, and the sediment settles on to the floor.

In the right places and amounts some sediments are very pleasant – the sand on the beach. The mud and slime of a bog or that left behind by a flood are not so enjoyable. Although these deposits do not much resemble rock, they are the kind of material from which most of the rocks now exposed at the surface of the earth were formed. Such layers of sand, clay or gravel can become consolidated in time to give those new formations called sedimentary rocks.

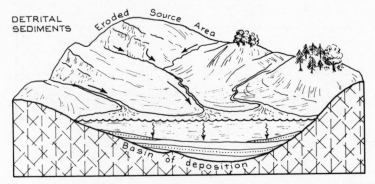

DETRITAL
SEDIMENTS

Weathered from parent rock, sediment is washed or blown into rivers, lakes or the sea where eventually it settles to the bottom. Layers of sediment accumulate and in time form sedimentary strata made largely of little bits of *detrital* material. The growing load of sediment compacts the material deposited earlier into sedimentary rock.

The change from loose sediment to firm rock can be brought about in several ways. Sand grains may be cemented together by mineral matter left behind by water trickling through the spaces between the grains. Muds and clays are in most cases changed into rock by the pressure of overlying deposits. This compresses the tiny grains together. Deeply buried sediments suffer a great deal of pressure and may also be baked by terrestrial heat. Under these conditions chemical changes may occur to harden the rock further.

Some rock formations, such as rock salt, are made up of minerals left behind when masses of water evaporated. Other sedimentary rocks contain great quantities of shells, or other skeletal remains, or plant fragments.

Just as there are two kinds of process to decompose rocks, so there are two ways in which sedimentary rocks can be formed. The products of physical weathering give us the *clastic* or *detrital rocks*, while chemical deposits give *chemical sedimentary rocks*. Most sedimentary rocks, however, have detrital fragments in them as well as some chemical or precipitated material.

The great common characteristic that all varieties of sedimentary rocks have is their layered or stratified structure. Each layer, or bed, or stratum, has a surface which was produced when the material was first deposited. It is called a bedding plane.

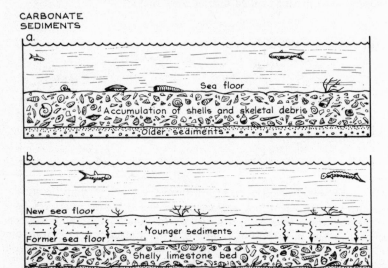

Most *limestones* seem to originate from the accumulation of lime-containing fragments from once living things: **a**, shells and skeletal debris composed of calcium carbonate accumulate on the sea floor: **b**, later sediments compress this bed of shelly material and help the slow process of consolidation and recrystallization of the smaller skeletal particles to form a limestone. (After Fagan).

DEPOSITION OF SEDIMENTS

Rock and mineral fragments – or, indeed, any non-floating solid material – is deposited when the transporting agent no longer has enough energy for the task. The faster a stream flows, the more energy it has and the greater the load of sediment it can carry. As it loses speed, a river loses energy and has to drop some of its load. The heaviest

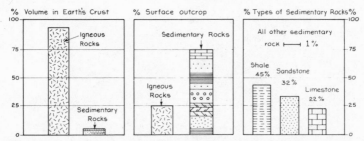

Different kinds and abundances of sedimentary rocks. Although over 95% of the outermost 15 km of the earth's crust is made of igneous rocks, sedimentary rocks cover three quarters of the continental areas of the world. We discount metamorphic rocks, considering them as igneous or sedimentary, depending on their origins.

particles are dropped first; when the water is at a standstill only the smallest or lightest particles remain suspended in it. In time even the finest particles may settle. Winds may follow the same action. In deserts light winds may whip up dust, but a really strong blast is needed to pick up such heavy objects as grains of sand. Soluble minerals, of course, may be carried along in solution until something causes them to be precipitated.

The places where sediments come to rest are called the environments of deposition. The conditions there largely control the kind of sediment that accumulates. On the bed of a swift upland stream, for example, only coarse sand and gravel may be deposited. The finer silt and sand is carried down to the lowland river plain, and much may not be deposited until the river sluggishly glides into a lake or the sea. Even there, however, tides, currents, waves and other disturbances may keep the sediment on the move.

Our diagram gives some idea of a few of the different environments of deposition which exist for sedimentary rocks.

MINERALS IN SEDIMENTARY ROCKS

Just three materials make up the bulk of sedimentary rocks – clay, quartz and calcite. They are the sedimentary rock-forming minerals, and in most of these rocks they all occur together. A few formations may consist of only one or other of this trio: limestones are made predominantly of calcite; quartzite or sandstone has little but quartz in it, and most clays have little calcite or quartz.

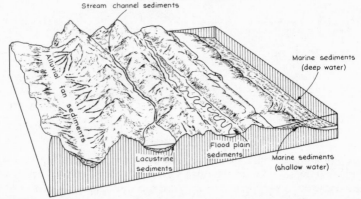

Areas where sedimentary rocks may accumulate. Most sediment is being deposited in the sea but some is left in scattered areas on land. The greater part of sediment derived from the land is dropped in shallow water near the shore. Only a small proportion reaches deep water. On the land, sediment may be deposited along stream and river channels and flood plains, in lakes and in alluvial fans at the foot of steep slopes and hills. (After Fagan).

Clay is really a whole family of minerals rather than one single type, and clay minerals are produced largely by the decomposition of the feldspars. The clay minerals have been rather difficult to identify since they form such tiny particles, but X-ray and other instrumental means of recognizing them have been developed. Quartz in its many different forms such as flint, chalcedony or chert, is very common. Few rocks have no quartz at all. Most of the quartz in sedimentary rocks is detrital, but it also occurs as a precipitate of very tiny crystals cementing other mineral grains together.

Calcite, however, is the most common cement in the coarser-grained sedimentary rocks. It is, as we saw in Chapter 2, a remarkable mineral in many ways, not least being its connection with living organisms. The action of carbonic acid on the calcium-bearing feldspars and some ferromagnesian minerals is to leach away the calcium as a soluble bicarbonate. The bicarbonate is rather easily induced to precipitate the insoluble carbonate, calcite. Many different animals and a few plants have adopted calcite to make hard structures – shells, skeletons, teeth, and the like.

Most limestones contain smaller quantities of another carbonate – dolomite, the double carbonate of calcium and magnesium. It is much less easily attacked by weathering than is calcite, and it is not common in shells.

Bits of feldspar and mica are abundant in some sedimentary rocks, and even pieces of ferromagnesian mineral may survive the hazards of weathering, transport and deposition. Rocks with detrital feldspar, mica, etc. are those which result from the products of physical rather than chemical weathering. Many were formed in deserts where there was little water to decompose the minerals.

Another constituent of most sedimentary rocks is iron. Produced by the chemical weathering of ferromagnesian minerals in igneous rocks, iron oxides are incorporated in sediments. Very many of the red, brown, yellow and greenish colours in sedimentary rocks are produced by quite small quantities of these metallic oxides.

Finally, we should note that organically produced matter, other than calcite, may be present. Coal is a sedimentary rock almost entirely made of plant materials, but it is more common for sedimentary rocks to contain only a little organic matter, and that sparsely scattered throughout the rock.

TEXTURE

The particles making up a sedimentary rock may be large or small, round or angular, long and thin or short and stubby, and they can be arranged in countless different ways. The general physical appearance they give to a rock is called its *texture*. There are two kinds of texture found in sedimentary rocks – the *clastic* and the *nonclastic*.

Clastic texture is shown by rocks made of fragments of mineral or rock. The name, clastic, refers to this broken or fragmental character. A coarse clastic rock might, for example, result from the gravels laid down on a beach or river bed, while a fine clastic rock could be produced from the mud on a lake floor or the dust blown across a desert. Clastic texture can be seen in chemical sedimentary rocks, and many a fossiliferous limestone consists of fragments of countless shells or other organic structures.

To help classify sedimentary rocks we may refer to the size of the individual grains or particles present. Most of these grains or particles have highly irregular shapes, but geologists assume that the majority of grains are more spherical than plate or needle-shaped and so they refer to them as having a 'diameter'. It is a useful way of arriving at an approximate measurement of particle size. The table shown here is the one in general use these days, and to determine the size of particles reasonably well it is usual to pass them through a set of sieves of known hole diameters.

Many a sedimentary rock seems to be made of crystals or fragments which are interlocked. They have an appearance rather similar to some igneous rocks with crystalline texture. Most sedimentary rocks of a chemical origin have a *nonclastic texture* and a crystalline structure.

The mineral crystals making these rocks have in most cases been precipitated from sea water. They are usually very small in size to begin with. As time passes, these crystals may grow by drawing more mineral matter from the solutions trapped in the original sediment. Eventually the crystals may form the bulk of the rock and each will interlock with its neighbours. Where the grains are larger in diameter than 5 mm the rock is said to be of coarse-grained texture. Fine-grained textures involve crystals or grains less than 1 mm in diameter.

Wentworth* Scale

Size of (hole) diameter	Fragment
	Boulder
256 mm	
	Cobble
64 mm	
	Pebble
4 mm	
	Granule
2 mm	
	Sand
1/16 mm	
	Silt
1/256 mm	
	Clay

* An American geologist who first used this scale of sizes.

LITHIFICATION

So far we have seen what are the raw materials needed to produce sedimentary rocks and how they may be brought into an environment of deposition. To convert the sediment into a consolidated, coherent rock involves the processes of *lithification*. It is a complicated affair in detail, but broadly there are four ways in which sediment may become lithified. Usually the final product is the result of several of these operating at the same time.

In many coarse-grained sedimentary rocks the spaces between the

PLATE 7. Igneous rocks commonly produce striking land forms, even where their formation long preceded the evolution of the landscape. *Above*, a granite mountain-side near Ben Nevis, Lochaber. *Below*, a volcanic vent filled with agglomerate and basalt which has cut through Carboniferous sedimentary rocks in the foreground. Dumgoyn, Scotland.

PLATE 8. Haytor, a famous landmark on Dartmoor, shows typical granite jointing and is well known for its large crystals of white orthoclase feldspar.

grains are filled by *cement*. Calcite, iron oxide, silica, anhydrite and
pyrite all act in this capacity and seem to have been spread through the
pore spaces of the rock by percolating water. Something within the
rock or during its history has caused the cement to be precipitated
from solution. When sedimentary rocks weather, it is in most cases
this cement which is removed in solution.

When a rock is *compacted* the pore spaces between the individual
grains are gradually reduced in size by the pressure of the overlying
sediments. Coarse-grained rocks seem to have suffered little compac-
tion, but fine-grained deposits of silt or clays can become compacted
to an appreciable degree. Some clays are thought to have had their
grains pressed closer and closer together when buried to depths of
1000 m or so to the extent of being compacted to about 60% of their
original volume.

The loss of pore space in a rock means that the water it contains is
squeezed out, and this *desiccation* may render the rock more cohesive,
just as it does when a soft mud is baked hard by the sun.

Finally, *crystallization* may take place. This may involve a reaction
between cement and grains, and indeed many cements are crystalline.
New minerals may form within the sedimentary rock after lithification
has begun, or some old mineral grains may grow at the expense of the
cement or of other grains. In the finer grained rocks particularly is it
seen that a whole range of new minerals may arise by recrystallization.
Much of this process is only poorly understood.

·TYPES OF SEDIMENTARY ROCKS

The seemingly endless variety of sedimentary rocks is one of their
attractions – or handicaps, according to your point of view. The
classification which most geologists use is rather a compromise affair.
It would be nice if the classification throughout reflected the origin
of the rocks, but the names given to most sedimentary rocks were in
use long before there were geologists!

The table below shows a classification commonly in use. Rocks are
thought of here as having a detrital, chemical or biochemical origin,
but in fact many rocks combine all three. Particle size is used to subdivide the detrital rocks and composition is used to subdivide the
chemical rocks. In recent years it has been found that one can use
particle size and nature to help classify many different limestones.

DETRITAL SEDIMENTARY ROCKS

Conglomerate. Made up of more or less rounded fragments, the majority of which are of granule size or larger, conglomerate may include materials of widely different origins. The larger fragments may be of different kinds of rock, but the smaller are mostly minerals derived from pre-existing rocks. Where the fragments are more angular than rounded the rock is called a *breccia.* Most conglomerates are formed from sediments deposited by powerful streams or by accumulation near the sea-shore or from deposits carried along by glacier ice.

Sandstone. In sandstones the grains are between 2 mm and one-sixteenth of a millimetre in diameter, but there may be rare pebbles or granules of larger size or seams of finer material present. We speak of coarse-grained, medium-grained or fine-grained sandstone, depending upon the predominant grain size. Where there is a wide range of grain shape and size the rock is said to be poorly sorted.

Quartz is the most common mineral in this group of sedimentary rocks, and where there is little else but quartz present in the rock it is called a *quartzose* sandstone. A sandstone rich in feldspar grains is said to be an *arkose.* Another common sandstone type is *greywacke,* a hard, dark rock rich in angular grains of quartz, feldspar and tiny rock fragments set in a matrix of clay-sized particles. Most, but not all, sandstones are rough to the touch, many contain fossils, and not a few are remarkably tough and long-lasting building stones.

Sandstones form from sandy sediment and this can be deposited in an enormous variety of environments – river-beds, lakes, swamps, deltas, sea-shores, lagoons, and even in deep ocean waters.

Siltstone, Mudstone and Shale. In this group of sedimentary rocks the sedimentary materials are predominantly of particles less than one-sixteenth of a millimetre in diameter. Clay figures very largely in their composition, but quartz silt is present in many, giving a roughness to the feel of the rock. *Mudstones* are massive or blocky rocks; *shales,* however, split into sheets and thin slabs more or less parallel to the bedding.

The mineralogical and chemical composition of these clayey or *argillaceous* rocks may vary widely, and the rocks are difficult to analyse except in a well-equipped laboratory. The individual particles may not be visible to the naked eye and even under a microscope they may not be identifiable. In addition to clay minerals and tiny quartz fragments there may be clay grade particles of feldspar, calcite, dolomite and iron ores. The list of ingredients is very long.

Clay grade particles can stay suspended in water for a very long time and clay deposits are thought to have formed in still or only gently moving water, or at great depths below the reach of waves or most currents. Much of the ocean floor is covered by clay-grade deposits, largely of material of wind-borne origin.

Because of the tiny size of the particles in these sediments they preserve very closely the outlines of shells or other objects buried in them. When the sediment is converted to rock the included organic material may perish, but the mould of its shape may be faithfully preserved down to the finest detail.

CHEMICAL ROCKS

There are in fact few rocks that are entirely of chemical origin and without any trace of detrital material. We have already looked at anhydrite, gypsum and halite, which are true chemical rocks, but the chemical rock that is of the greatest volume is undoubtedly limestone.

Limestones are an immensely important group of sedimentary rocks. They consist of calcium carbonate (calcite) with minor quantities of other minerals. The calcite has been deposited by either inorganic or organic processes. Some years ago it was thought that the greater part of the earth's limestones were of inorganic origin. Nowadays we recognize the essential role of many different kinds of living organisms in producing most new deposits of lime sediment. A clastic texture is characteristic of most limestones, but crystalline nonclastic textures occur in some.

Organic activity in the formation of limestones involves the extraction of calcium carbonate from the water surrounding them. Corals, molluscs and others use the hard calcite or aragonite in their skeletons. Some primitive plants precipitate layers of calcite as part of their normal activity. From the accumulations of the skeletal parts of such organisms we have shell banks, coral reefs, and algal banks. Algae have been producing calcium carbonate since Precambrian times; most of the others began to use it in early Palaeozoic days. Fossil coral reefs, much like modern reefs in many ways, are known from rocks as early as the Ordovician. For the most part, it is the tropical seas that support the largest numbers of lime-secreting organisms. Corals are

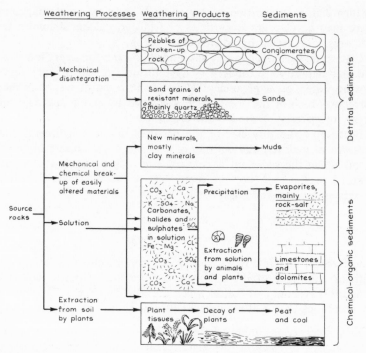

Broad outline of the origins of the two main divisions of sedimentary rocks. (After Read and Watson).

restricted today to latitudes below 30 degrees north or south and where the water is shallow. Here, too, inorganic precipitation of carbonate may take place at times when its concentration in the water reaches saturation point, but mostly it seems to be the result of the chemical activity of algae and invertebrate animals. A key factor in the control of carbonate precipitation is the concentration of carbon dioxide in the water. When the concentration goes below a critical level the carbonate is deposited. Seaweeds are active in removing carbon-dioxide from the water as part of their normal chemical activity in sunlight, in the process known as photosynthesis. They feed by turning carbon dioxide and water into sugars and so the amount of carbon dioxide in sea water may vary with the activity of the plants locally present in the sea. When they are numerous enough and active enough, calcium carbonate is precipitated as an inorganic by-product of the biological activity.

PLATE 9. Structures within volcanic rocks. *Above*, columnar jointing in basalt of Tertiary (Cainozoic) age, Northern Ireland. *Below*, nodular rhyolitic lava of the Ordovician Bala Volcanic Series, Gwynedd.

PLATE 10. Veins and intrusive rock bodies range from microscopic to gigantic. *Above left,* quartz veins in sandstone; *right,* pyrite veins in slate; *below left,* pegmatite in granite; *right,* quartz-porphyry in slate.

Nearly all limestones have been formed in the sea. The water in lakes and rivers tend to contain acids in sufficient quantities to prevent the precipitation of calcium carbonate. For the same reason, perhaps, lime-secreting organisms such as shellfish are much more abundant in the sea than in rivers and lakes.

One form of limestone which is quite distinctive is *oolite*, and its coarse variety pisolite (pea-stone). Oolite resembles cod-roe in appearance, being made up of tiny spheres of calcium carbonate. Each sphere or oolith has a tiny nucleus consisting of a silt or shell particle around which layers of carbonate have been deposited. These layers are added as the nucleus is rolled about by tides and currents on the sea floor in much the same way as a snowball grows when it is rolled over wet snow.

Travertine, calcareous tufa and *dripstone* are local deposits of inorganically precipitated limestone, more often than not they are associated with caves. Stalactites and stalagmites are formed where water evaporates from a drip point at the point where it lands on the cave floor. Travertine is characteristically full of cavities and hollows either where no lime was deposited or where it was subsequently redissolved away.

Dolomite, or as it is sometimes called, *dolostone*, is a rock which consists largely of the mineral dolomite which we examine in Chapter 6. The origin of this rock has worried geologists for a long time. Only a very little dolomite ever seems to be directly precipitated in the warmer seas. Organisms do not appear to use it in skeletal structures and yet dolomite is common among the sedimentary rocks. There are vast quantities of it in the Palaeozoic systems and even in the Precambrian. Nearly all dolomites are presumed to have formed from the replacement of limestone. Somehow the calcium-magnesium carbonate formed in place of the simple calcium carbonate – so the magnesium had to be introduced from somewhere. It represents a little over 3.5% of all the solids dissolved in sea water so presumably that is where it comes from to react with the calcium carbonate. Even so, we cannot say exactly when the change takes place. Perhaps it immediately follows deposition, perhaps it comes much later. When it does take place, dolomitization so reorganizes the texture of the rock that it destroys nearly all the fossils and, no doubt, many other features too.

SEDIMENTARY TRADEMARKS

Even with the use of the hand-lens which every good geologist carries in the field, it is difficult to decide what materials a rock specimen may contain. Some igneous, metamorphic and sedimentary rocks have very much the same appearance, but there may be clues to their nature, as for example fossils, outcrop pattern or sedimentary structures.

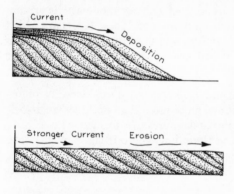

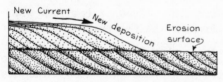

The origin of cross-bedding, also known as cross-stratification or false-bedding. Where sand is deposited in dunes by the wind the entire dune shape may be preserved.

When a sediment is deposited it may be influenced by local movements in the air or water which cause irregularities in the way in which the particles settle. An obvious example is the to-and-fro lap of the waves in shallow water; the rippled surface of the water seems to be mirrored by a similarly rippled surface on the soft mud or sand beneath. *Ripple-marks* are a form of sedimentary structure. So, too, in a way are some *trace fossils*, the origins of which are mentioned in Chapter 8.

Perhaps the most universal features of all sedimentary rocks are the bedding planes which mark the former surface of the sea floor or lake or other site where sedimentation was taking place. They persist in the sedimentary rock either because the beds above and below are slightly different in composition and texture, or because the one below had time to settle and compact slightly before the next was laid down. Fossils are for the most part found on bedding planes rather than within the beds. Bedding planes can be many feet apart, but others are

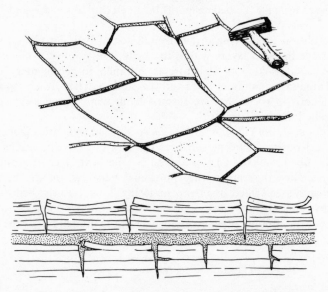

Desiccation cracks occur in muds and silty rocks when they dry out under the sun. Later coverings of sand or silt may preserve them. The lower figure shows sun-dried and cracked (mud) shales covered by a sand layer which preserves the polygonal pattern seen in the figure above.

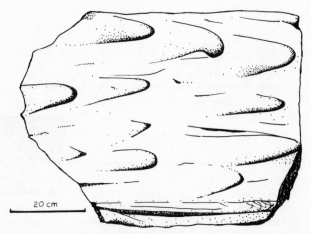

On the under surfaces of many sandstones are preserved the impressions in reverse of hollows and grooves scoured by currents prior to the deposition of the sandy bed itself. These are often called flute casts and groove casts and may range from tiny to gigantic in size.

so close as to make the beds paper thin. Such thin layers are sometimes called *laminae*.

In addition to showing originally horizontal bedding planes, some rocks have inclined layers within the beds; these are *cross-laminae* or *cross-beds*. This kind of structure is common in sedimentary rocks found along the margin of lakes and seas and in deltas. It is even more conspicuous in rocks that are formed from wind-blown sand and is then called *dune-bedding*.

Mud-cracks, sun-cracks or *desiccation-cracks* are structures that result when a deposit of mud or silt dries out and cracks. The cracks may later be filled, covered and preserved by the next layer of sediment. In appearance they are mostly polygonal networks on the bedding planes with small filled fissures penetrating down into the bed below.

Many sedimentary rocks have irregular under-surfaces which represent the infilling of an erosion surface, the eroded top of the rock

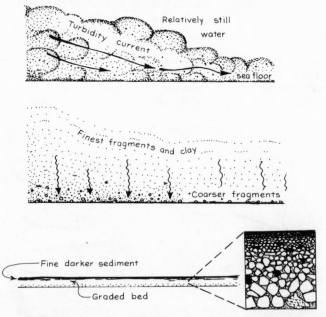

Some beds, commonly muddy sandstones, have a very regular distribution of the grains with the largest at the bottom. Such beds are sometimes called *turbidites* and were deposited from turbulent currents of sand suspended in muddy water as shown above. Turbidites may cover hundreds of square kilometres; tiny ones can occur in garden ponds.

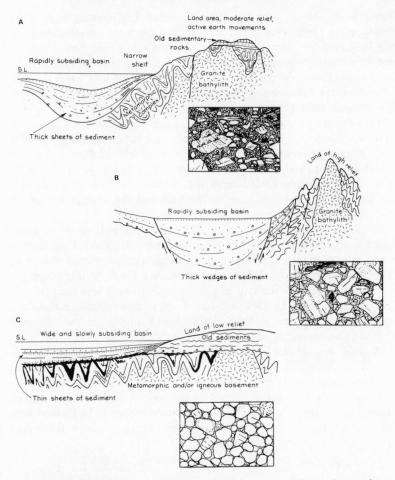

A, Muddy, dark, hard sandstones, *greywackes,* occur in regions where mountains or uplands rapidly shed sediment on to a nearby subsiding sea floor. They contain angular rock and mineral fragments in a matrix of dark clayey mineral matter. Fossils are rare. B, Red or pale coloured sandstones with lots of feldspar grains and fragments are called *arkoses* and are derived from upland areas and deposited on land rather than in the sea. Most are not very fossiliferous but some have the bones of land animals. C, Very pure quartz sandstones, or *orthoquartzites,* result from sands that accumulated slowly, during which time all the chemically destructible minerals are removed. The well-rounded quartz grains are commonly about the same size. The insets are magnified 8–10 times.

beneath. In others, however, rather similar irregularities have been produced by plastic contortion of the surface between a mud and a sand not long after the overlying sand was deposited. These *flow structures* are produced by the movement of water and sediment in response to little local changes of pressure within them. If the whole mass is tilted by some movement the sloppy material may even flow and bulge downhill, further deforming the plane between sand and mud.

In sedimentary rocks deposited in rather deep water we may find *graded bedding* with a graduation of grain size from top to bottom of a bed. This is in many cases the result of a muddy (turbidity) current which brought in all grades of material from very coarse to very fine. The larger particles settled most rapidly and the finer more slowly. So we have grains of all sizes in the bed, but the coarser are at the bottom and the finer at the top.

Some sedimentary rocks contain structures formed after the sediment was deposited. They include *concretions* and *geodes*. Concretions form as local concentrations of cementing material within the rock. They may form around a nucleus such as a fossil or large mineral grain and are most abundant in porous formations where the cement-carrying solutions can move around. Most commonly concretions are spherical or disc-like. Calcite, limonite and quartz are the minerals that are the cementing agents in most cases.

Nodules are similar in some respects but are inclined to be less regular in shape. They may be masses of silica (*flint* is a good example) or other minerals that have chemically replaced parts of limestones.

Geodes look like concretions but are hollow and have linings of inward-projecting crystals. The hollow or cavity has to be formed first and the crystals grow from solutions introduced later. Calcite and quartz geodes can be very beautiful.

CHAPTER 6

EVAPORATE TO DRYNESS:
SALT AND EVAPORITES

NOT all minerals are associated with volcanic heat and great pressure within the crust of the earth or with the formation of veins and lodes beneath the surface. Many minerals are rather soluble in water and a few are extremely easily dissolved. It is with these very soluble earth materials that we are concerned in this chapter. Most of them are deposited in one form or another when water evaporates or when slight chemical changes occur within it, be it sea water, water in a hot spring, or in a cave.

As you might expect, the biggest bodies of water, the oceans, have the largest total amounts and range of minerals dissolved in them. They contain all the common elements and most of the uncommon ones in solution or suspension. In its own way the sea is a great treasure-house of materials which every day becomes more attractive to mineral-hungry nations. There are schemes of varying degrees of ingenuity and costliness for mining, collecting or chemically extracting minerals from the sea-bed or from the waters themselves.

As the evolution of the earth has progressed so the positions and size of many of the ancient seas have changed. Climate has changed too. In several cases large areas of shallow sea have become cut off from the oceans and have dried up, leaving minerals and salts behind. The sands and muds of time covered up these deposits, evaporites, only to have them unearthed long after or probed by deep wells.

THE SALTS

Of all the minerals that man uses every day and would hate to be without, salt is the commonest and most important. For those who live within reach of the sea it is available in plenty, but for peoples far inland there is nearly always the problem of where to get this vital mineral. In the ancient world there was an important traffic in salt along the trade and caravan routes. Some inland regions, in Africa, North America and Asia especially, have salt lakes and brine springs, but they are for the most part rather inhospitable areas.

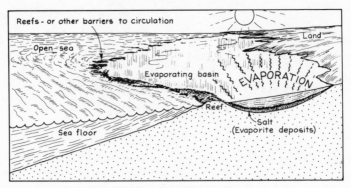

An origin for salt deposits. At the edge of the sea in regions of low rainfall reefs or other barriers may restrict the free movement of the water. A natural evaporating basin is produced and gypsum, salt and other soluble minerals may be precipitated as the water evaporates away.

Salt, the familiar sodium chloride, is the compound to give its name to a whole family of chemical substances, the salts. These we may define as compounds of metallic ions and ions such as chlorine (Cl), iodine (I), sulphate (SO_4) and others. Most of them are soluble in water and are chemically very active, their ions seeming anxious to enter a great variety of bondings with others.

In their crystalline forms salts adopt many beautiful shapes and some are beautifully coloured, especially the salts of copper, iron and some other metals. Because they dissolve so easily in water few of them are commonly found at the surface of the earth unless the climate is very dry, unless volcanic activity is taking place, or because of other rare circumstances. Nevertheless, they turn up in small quantities in many unexpected places. Being soluble, salts are found in small quantities in many of the lakes, streams and rivers of the world. For the most part they are present in such small amounts that they escape notice, but many springs and waters have a peculiar, in many cases unpleasant, taste once they contain these chemicals. More than a few naturally gassy 'mineral waters' have an appreciable content of these soluble minerals.

All waters seem ultimately to find their way to the sea, and it is no wonder to us that they have in the course of time carried a tremendous quantity of salts into the seas and oceans of the world. Such salts have made the briny ocean what it is. The commonest salt in the sea by far is sodium chloride, common salt, or *halite* as it is known. From the

PLATE 11. Clastic or fragmental rocks: *top left,* a closely packed pebble
conglomerate (×.25); *right,* conglomeratic sandstone (×.25); *centre left,* a
volcanic breccia or agglomerate (×.25); *right,* a sedimentary breccia
(×.25); *below left,* close-up of a coarse 'sharp' quartz sandstone. (×4);
right, close-up of a medium 'shell' sandstone (×2).

PLATE 12. *Above,* well-bedded and jointed sandstones and shales give rise to striking cliff forms. Corbyn Head, S. Devon. *Below,* sole-structures on a sandstone which overlay soft shale. Shale is caught up between adjacent lobes of sandstone. N. Devon.

sea then is it most easily recovered, but many countries nowadays obtain salts, halite and others, from deposits below the ground. When enormous deposits of sylvite (potassium chloride, KCl) were found under the Canadian prairies some years ago they were more welcome than gold – and much more useful. An echo of the Canadian cheers rose in northern England not long after, for potassium minerals were discovered below ground there also.

So important are such natural resources to the chemical industry of a modern nation that a great deal of effort goes into locating and developing likely deposits. In the 1960s the world total of salt produced each year was about 100,500,000 short tons. Nearly threequarters of all the salt produced is used as a chemical raw material for industry. Most of it, however, came not from the sea, the obvious source, but from underground deposits.

HALITE

Before we look further at the ways in which the different salts occur geologically we should examine halite a little further. It illustrates a number of interesting things mineralogically and it has played an important part in the history of modern crystal chemistry. Halite was in fact the first substance to be investigated, and its crystal structure determined, by X-rays by the Cambridge physicist W. L. Bragg. He was interested to examine the structure of a simple compound rather than that of an element. Salt seemed a good choice, a compound in which two ions, Na^+ and Cl^-, are linked or bonded. In rock salt each sodium ion seems to be surrounded by six chlorine ions and vice-versa. This produces a cubic arrangement of ions as shown on page 21, and the common crystalline form of this substance is a cube. Halite also has a cubic cleavage and the low hardness (2.5 on Mohs' scale) reflects the weak attractive forces between the large ions. Pure halite is transparent and this, we believe, is because there are no free electrons in the halite structure to interfere with the various wavelengths of incoming light. The streak of halite is white and the mineral has the most distinctive taste of all.

SALTS IN THE SEA

All seas are salty and some are extremely so. The normal salt content is 35 parts per thousand, but in areas of very hot dry climate evaporation removes the water from the sea and the concentration of salts rises.

In the Red Sea it is 40 parts per thousand, and in the Dead Sea the concentration, more than 40 parts per thousand, is too high to allow most forms of marine life to exist. But sodium chloride is not the only salt in the sea. Normal sea water has the following principal constituents dissolved in it.

		Grams per 100 grams of water
Sodium chloride	NaCl	23
Magnesium chloride	$MgCl_2$	5
Sodium sulphate	$NaSO_4$	4
Calcium chloride	$CaCl_2$	1
Potassium chloride	KCl	0.7
With other minor ingredients to total		34.5

34.5 is said to be the *salinity* of the sea water.

Knowing how much salt and other solubles there are in the sea water and that each year rivers add to it, geologists have wondered if they could deduce from these facts how old the oceans are. Today, we believe, the total annual supply of dissolved material poured into the sea by streams around the world is some 3,600,000,000,000,000 grams. Despite all those o's, the arithmetic should be simple, but the answer seems to be a ridiculously short period of time. A proposal to investigate the age of the earth by this method was proposed as long ago as 1715 by the astronomer Edmund Halley. Late in the nineteenth century calculations were produced to show that about 90 million years had passed since water first condensed on the earth and began to dissolve salts. A basic difficulty in this kind of argument is that we do not know if the rate at which salt is added to the sea by rivers and streams carrying it from the land is the same today as it was long ago. Sodium, or salt, liberated from rocks during weathering and decomposition simply does not accumulate indefinitely in the sea. Some of it is removed by the wind in sea spray, some is buried with sediments (see page 92). So there is a sort of balance established. These give-and-take processes have probably not changed much since Precambrian days.

SOME OTHER EVAPORITES

Although halite is a remarkable and abundant evaporite it is not the only one commonly found among the sedimentary rocks. The list of

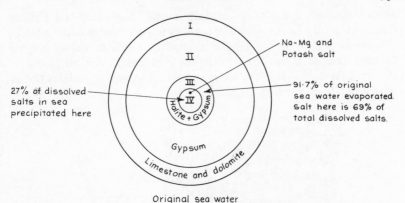

Successive stages in the evaporation of sea water. If we evaporate a quantity of sea water the relative volume of brine during each stage of precipitation can be represented by the series of circles like water levels in an evaporating basin.

salts in the sea quoted above gives a few others, and there are more. Of these, only calcium sulphate, in its mineral forms *anhydrite* and *gypsum,* is much in evidence. It is found in many parts of the world; the others are for one reason or another much more local in their occurrence.

Anhydrite is the simple compound calcium sulphate, $CaSO_4$, crystallizing in prisms or in tabular forms of the orthorhombic system. In many cases it is fibrous or granular and compact. It has a good cleavage in three directions, giving rectangular fragments. Anhydrite is white when pure but may acquire attractive blue, grey or reddish tints. The cleavage planes have a pearly or vitreous lustre, but the mineral often has an uneven fracture. It is rather soft, 3–3.5 on Mohs' scale; and it has a low specific gravity, 2.93.

There are many varieties of anhydrite and it is locally found associated and mixed with hydrated calcium sulphate, gypsum, $CaSO_4 . 2H_2O$. The two minerals are found interbanded in many deposits, which is of interest because anhydrite forms from gypsum in sea water when the temperature reaches 25°C and when the salinity reaches a critical level. So possibly the alternating layers may be annual deposits.

Gypsum, not unexpectedly, is like anhydrite in many respects, but it crystallizes in distinctive forms in the monoclinic system. It occurs for the most part in radiating clumps of needle-like or fibrous crystals or as laminated, granular or compact masses. *Satin spar* is a fibrous form with a silky lustre; *alabaster* is a very fine-grained massive variety. *Selenite* is a clear rather tabular crystalline form as shown below. In large crystals it has a good cleavage giving thin, flexible plates or slivers. Like anhydrite, it is white or colourless but sometimes tinted with a pearly or vitreous lustre.

Anhydrite and its relative gypsum, calcium sulphate, take on many forms. In veins and cavities infillings of fibrous or needle-shaped crystals of gypsum may produce what is sometimes termed 'satin spar' (*left*). Single crystals of calcium sulphate, known as selenite (*right*), are common in many clay formations. Alabaster is a very fine-grained massive variety.

About 10 million tons of anhydrite and gypsum are excavated each year and 90% of this goes into building materials. The rest is used in the chemical industry to make paints, fertilizers, weed killers, and many other useful products.

Nitrates are soluble minerals with rather a restricted distribution. Sodium nitrate from the desert in the northern regions of Chile in South America make up about 80% of the world production. Nitrates are interesting in that they are believed to originate when organic matter is oxidized in the presence of sodium or potassium salts and certain bacteria.

Borax and *natron* are also salts of sodium which are found in desert regions and in areas far from the sea. They seem to be derived from the weathering of certain igneous rocks, being leached out of them by the occasional heavy rains of spring. Hot springs and volcanic activity may result in crusts of borax-like minerals being formed around gas and steam vents.

THE ORIGINS OF EVAPORITE DEPOSITS

When part of the sea or any large body of water dries up the salts once dissolved in it are left behind. A hot dry climate is needed to speed

PLATE 13. *Above*, dune-bedding in New Red Sandstone at Mauchline Quarries, Strathclyde, a famous photograph of a famous locality. *Below*, cross-bedding in a Precambrian sandstone, showing that currents flowed from left to right.

PLATE 14. *Above left,* a fine-grained rock resembling shale and claystone but which in fact is stratified soft volcanic dust. Stirling. *Right,* ripple-marked sandstone from an ancient lake floor. Orkney. *Below,* these parallel lines are not traces of bedding but the deceptive marks made by ice-borne debris moving from right to left across the exposed rock.

along the drying process and as the water evaporates the concentration of the dissolved minerals rises. Fish and other creatures may be killed off when this happens. Salt begins to appear around the edges of the shrinking lagoon or lake.

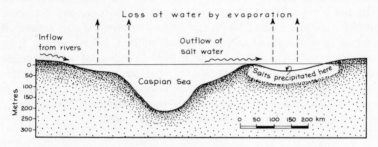

Cross section of the Gulf of Kara Borghaz. (After Holmes).

A very good example of this kind of happening is in the Gulf of Kara Borghaz on the east side of the Caspian Sea. It is a hot dry part of the southern U.S.S.R. where evaporation in the shallow gulf is so high that over the last forty years the water level has been actually lowered below that in the nearby sea. A current permanently flowing into the Gulf is set up through the narrow inlet which connects the gulf and sea. The current brings in more and more salts in solution. In the Gulf it is evaporated and the precipitated minerals sink to the floor. A thick layer of salts, mostly sodium sulphate, is being built up and gives a situation like those we find among ancient sedimentary deposits.

The law of solubility states that the least soluble materials are precipitated first. In lagoons and gulfs where sea water is evaporating, the sequence of salts deposited is a complex response to temperature, pressure, relative solubilities and other factors. Laboratory experiments with sea water have given us some idea about the way in which it may happen. When the sea water is half boiled away calcium carbonate is precipitated along with a trace of iron and aluminium hydroxide. When the volume is reduced to about one-fifth, calcium sulphate appears. Sodium chloride, magnesium sulphate and magnesium chloride appear when the original volume is reduced to about one-tenth.

In nature all kinds of interruptions may take place during the evaporation process and many impurities such as wind-blown dust may be added to the salty precipitate. Many salt-bearing formations have a distinctive layering with the last formed layers (at the top) containing the most soluble salts, commonly those of potassium.

Famous salt deposits of this kind occur in Germany, northern England, New York State, and western Canada.

Potassium salts occur in those evaporite deposits which have resulted from the most extreme desiccation, since they are among the most soluble of all minerals. The annual tonnage produced and recovered in terms of potassium oxide is about four million. Nine-tenths of it go to making fertilizers and the rest is used in the glass and ceramics industry, and to make dyes, explosives, matches, photographic chemicals and many other necessary things. The most important and common potassium mineral salt is *sylvite*, potassium chloride, KCl. In many deposits sylvite is mixed with halite and other salts.

THE CARBONATES

Most of the rocks we have mentioned so far are made up of crystals or fragments of crystals. Beds of rock salt or other evaporites are composed very largely of one mineral, halite, or a relative of halite. Carbonate rocks are similarly monomineralic – consisting of one mineral for the most part. The mineral (or minerals) is calcium carbonate in the majority of cases and the rocks are *limestones*. Not uncommon, however, are rocks made of the double carbonate of calcium and magnesium, and they are known as *dolomites* or *dolostones*.

Carbonates are comparatively simple chemical compounds with metallic ions linked with carbonate ions, CO_3. The bonds between the ions are not as tough as those, for example, in many of the silicate minerals, and carbonates are rather more chemically active than the silicates. When silicates undergo weathering they may break down to

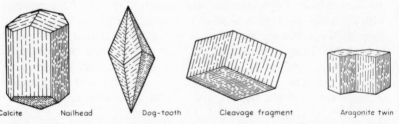

Calcite   Nailhead   Dog-tooth   Cleavage fragment   Aragonite twin

Calcite and aragonite are crystalline forms of calcium carbonate. Crystals of calcite are common but clearly identifiable aragonite is relatively rare. Twinned crystals are not uncommon.

produce quartz, clay and the hydroxides and carbonates of calcium, sodium and potassium. Quartz and clays make up large volumes of sedimentary rocks, and so under rather different circumstances do the carbonates.

While some limestones and dolomites are clearly sedimentary rocks made up of large particles of the carbonates, others seem to be chemical precipitates. Many limestones are composed of shells, coral skeletons or the limestone crusts secreted by algal plants. In fact, they owe their formation largely to the activity of living organisms. With the invention of more and more powerful microscopes we have been able to detect organic structures in very fine sediments indeed, sediments that we had previously thought of as chemical precipitates.

Before we look at the carbonate rocks it will be useful to say something about the minerals. Perhaps the most important and puzzling physical property these minerals have is their solubility in water. Normally it is very low, but calcium carbonate will dissolve readily in water that is acidic. Even the presence of a little dissolved carbon dioxide in water is enough to make the difference, and calcium carbonate becomes by reaction the soluble bicarbonate. Dolomite does not follow this example, however, and remains relatively insoluble. It must be said that dolomite is altogether rather hard to understand. While there are many parts of the world where calcite or its relative, *aragonite,* is being directly precipitated, it is difficult to locate dolomite forming in the same way. It seems that dolomite replaces the calcium carbonate in the sediment not long after that mineral has been deposited. Yet there are enormous rock formations composed of dolomite, especially among the early Palaeozoic systems, and in a few late-Precambrian groups.

Several geologists have sought to explain the absence of limestones from the earliest rocks known by suggesting that the early atmosphere was very rich in carbon dioxide. This would dissolve in the waters where sediments form and prevent any of the acid-soluble carbonates from being precipitated. Only later did oxygen replace the carbon dioxide and so allow limestone to accumulate.

CALCITE is the common, more or less transparent, or tinted form of calcium carbonate and is relatively abundant. Crystallizing in the hexagonal system, it has three main crystal forms; these are (1) nail-head spar – hexagonal prisms with rather flat three-faced ends; (2) dog-tooth spar which has hexagonal prisms and sharp, pointed ends; and (3) rhombohedral crystals with the appearance of lop-sided matchboxes. Some occurrences are very perfect beautiful crystals reaching a large size, but calcite also occurs in fibrous, lamellar, nodular and granular forms.

The cleavage is spectacularly regular, so that when calcite is broken it is always along the planes which form parallels to the rhombohedron.

Commonly prismatic calcite crystals occur in cavities in limestones and associated with mineral veins. Here are 'nail-head spar', 'dog-tooth spar' and the transparent 'Iceland spar' with its double refraction.

Even powdered calcite consists of minute cleavage rhombohedra. The colourless and transparent character of the mineral is usually masked by the presence of tiny impurities which make it white, brown, black, or red. Nevertheless, it has a white streak and a vitreous lustre. Easily scratched by a knife, its hardness on Mohs' scale is 3.

Perhaps the most distinctive optical property of very pure calcite is that of *double refraction*. It splits a beam of light into two parts as the light passes through so that a 'double image' is seen when an object is viewed through it. Iceland has provided some of the finest crystals of this kind of pure calcite, which is sometimes known as Iceland spar.

Satin spar is a compact, finely fibrous variety with a satin-like lustre. It is mostly to be found in veins and crevices in rocks with the fibres perpendicular to the walls. The name satin spar has also been used for fibrous gypsum.

ARAGONITE is another, less common, form of calcium carbonate; many occurrences also contain 1–2% of strontium carbonate. Like calcite in many ways, it nevertheless crystallizes in the orthorhombic system. The crystals may be twinned many times, needle-shaped, some resembling hexagonal crystals. In colour, lustre and hardness it resembles, but is not identical with, calcite, and to distinguish between the two can be difficult. Aragonite occurs with calcite and in beds of gypsum. It is also a form of carbonate produced by corals, algae and some shellfish. In sediments, however, it is soon converted to calcite, the principal cause of this change being the weight of the material above. For this reason aragonite is not commonly found in sedimentary rocks, though it may occur in veins and cavities, in cave stalactites and as a deposit around hot springs.

DOLOMITE, which has about 45% of its composition as magnesium carbonate, resembles its simpler relative, calcite. It is one of the very few minerals that have curved faces. Dolomite crystals belong to the hexagonal system, with a rhombohedral form the most common. Massive and granular forms also occur. Its lustre, hardness and specific gravity are all close to those of calcite, but it usually has a rather distinctive yellowish tinge and is rather brittle.

Dolomite, the double carbonate of magnesium and calcium, is not commonly found in large crystals, but where it is, it is recognizable by its curved crystal faces. (After Rutley).

The exact nature of this mineral is rather interesting, and it cannot be regarded as a magnesium-rich variety of calcite. Calcium ions appear to be larger than magnesium ions and so cannot be interchanged in crystal structures. What happens in the crystallization of calcite is that the ions are distributed as alternating layers of calcium ions and carbonate ions. In dolomite the magnesium ions take the place of every second calcium ion layer, so there are twice as many carbonate layers as calcium or magnesium layers.

CHAPTER 7

SUNDRY DISGUISES:
THE METAMORPHIC ROCKS

THE mountainous regions of the earth are exciting no less to the geologist than to the mountaineer or traveller. They are places where great changes have been taking place in the crust. We can see the ravages being wrought by snow and ice, wind and rain, and how land-slides, rock-falls and avalanches all help to wear down the mountains. The rocks exposed in these wild areas may show violent and peculiar contortions of strata, and there are many other signs that the mountains were compressed and raised up by great forces from within the crust. What the forces of the underworld pushed up, the spirits of water, ice and wind are wearing down.

This task of destruction is not made easy by the nature of the rocks themselves. At first glance one could mistake many of these rock formations for igneous bodies, composed of the familiar silicate minerals and quartz. But their crystals are arranged in a peculiar way, many being segregated into countless thin layers, glossy and shining. Other rocks seem to be more coarsely crystalline and uniform in composition and appearance. On closer inspection they are found to be made largely of calcite crystals or of quartz. These are all *metamorphic* rocks, changed from their original form by heat, pressure and chemi-cally active fluids in the course of time.

METAMORPHISM

These striking changes were brought about by the same forces that folded, fractured and raised up the rocks of the mountain ranges, and that perhaps injected igneous magma into the area. We have seen that as sediments are buried so they become hardened and cemented. Their physical character and even their chemical composition may change. The deeper the burial the more effective are the changes. As pressure increases, recrystallization and the formation of new minerals may take place. The new minerals in most cases are made of very closely packed atoms.

Recrystallization is produced in another way as well – by heat. When compressed very severely in a mountain chain a clayey rock may become hard, brittle and platey in appearance. But the same rock may turn into a very different metamorphic material when it is heated or baked by the heat of an igneous intrusion. It may change in colour and develop spots and new crystals visible to the naked eye. Intense baking will metamorphose it into a lustrous, tough, well-crystallized rock. This is what has happened around many granite intrusions such as that of the Skiddaw Granite, which has produced in the local Skiddaw Slates a series of changes in a zone about 800 m thick.

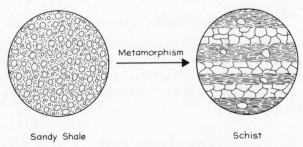

Sandy Shale   Schist

The metamorphism of sandy shale to a schist involves a reorganization of the mineralogical and textural characters of the rock. The sand grains become gathered into layers of crystalline quartz alternating with new materials, i.e. platy micas and scattered mineral crystals such as garnet. Magnified about 10 times. (After Laporte).

During these processes of metamorphism a great deal of reorganization of the texture and composition of the rock takes place. Fossils or sedimentary features such as ripple-marks may be destroyed or deformed in the process. Some rocks, especially the clays, shales and marls – called collectively the pelitic rocks – are metamorphosed comparatively easily. Others need much greater pressures or higher temperatures to make them change.

Of course if the temperatures and pressures in the rocks are pushed high enough, all minerals will eventually change or simply melt. A completely molten rock underground is what we know as magma. So metamorphism can only occur while the rock is not yet molten.

When a rock is buried to depths of 10,000 metres or more the pressure upon it may be 20,000 kilogrammes per square centimetre This is enough pressure to cause most rocks to become as plastic as toothpaste; their power to resist the forces pushing at them in the crust is overcome. Heating and squeezing affect not only the crystal grains within the rock but also the fluids in the pore spaces. These hot fluids can react with the local mineral grains and produce completely new minerals with characteristics quite different from those that were present before. In some instances the emplacement of an igneous magma has released hot mineral-rich fluids into the rocks round about, producing new suites of metamorphic, or as they are called in these cases, *metasomatic* minerals. They were mentioned in connection with the metallic ores on page 58.

TYPES OF METAMORPHISM

During the history of the earth there have been many different events to cause metamorphism. No doubt the processes are going on now just as they have in the past. We can broadly distinguish two basic types of metamorphism – contact metamorphism and regional metamorphism.

Contact metamorphism

Contact metamorphism is what happens to rock when hot magma is brought into contact with it. Scorching and baking may be part of the process, but in the case of rocks and magma deep underground other important changes take place too. To give an analogy, baked bread is not really like the dough that goes into the oven: the heat and the working of yeast change the material's form, yet the chemical composition does not change appreciably. Water and gas are removed by the heat. Bricks in a kiln also suffer a loss of water and gas, and the very high heat there actually causes reorganization of the mineral matter into new hard forms.

Underground it is not so easy for water and gas to escape from a heated rock. Another important factor makes itself felt there too. As we have seen, magma itself contains a lot of superheated gas and water vapour. At the contact between magma and surrounding rock these hot gases and solutions escape from the magma: they introduce new elements into the rock and carry away some of those originally there.

This replacement occurs naturally in a restricted zone or skin around the igneous rock. These *contact aureoles*, as they are called, are never more than a few hundred metres thick. Although some aureoles are only a few centimetres wide, they are always present no matter how big

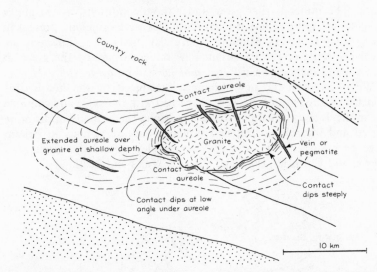

Sketch-map of a denuded granite intrusion and the aureole or halo of baked rock around it.

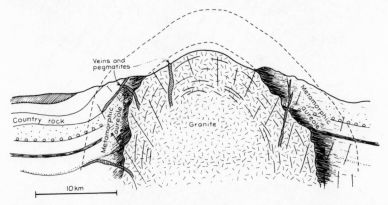

A granite intrusion, like that above, seen in cross-section. The intensity of the contact metamorphism diminishes outwards from the granite margin.

or small the intrusion of magma is. Experiments in the laboratory indicate that the temperatures in the aureoles may be as high as 680°C and pressures may reach 5000 atmospheres* when the intrusion takes

* One atmosphere is the pressure we normally experience at the earth's surface: it is measured in various ways.

place. The minerals that grow under these conditions, as we might imagine, are quite different from those that were originally present in the country rock. For example, where clay minerals or limestone are involved, some of the important new minerals may be the greenish calcium and magnesium silicates, *diopside* and *tremolite*.

We referred to the new minerals introduced by the hot hydrothermal solutions when we were concerned with the oxide and sulphide ore minerals and the gangue that accompanies them. Many of the more varied and interesting ores and minerals once so famous in Britain have been mined from the contact aureoles around the granites of Devon and Cornwall, the Lake District, Wales and Scotland.

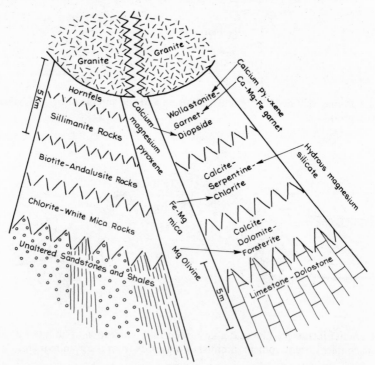

The kinds of new mineral assemblages that are created by the contact or thermal metamorphism around an igneous intrusion depend upon the nature of the rocks originally present. Limestones and detrital rocks pass through several stages, each with its characteristic minerals, as the metamorphism proceeds. The minerals requiring the highest temperatures for their formation are only found near the igneous rock body.

There are three aluminium silicates (Al_2SiO_5) which commonly occur in metamorphic rocks – *andalusite, sillimanite* and *kyanite*. All three are closely related and contain independent silica tetrahedra. In regions of contact metamorphism, andalusite and sillimanite are common, but kyanite forms in clayey rocks that are subjected to regional metamorphism, as we see below.

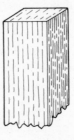 

Andalusite and chiastolite crystals are seldom more than a few millimetres long but they are common aluminium silicates produced by thermal metamorphism.

Andalusite   Chiastolite

Andalusite is a very distinctive mineral occurring in small pale brown, red, pink or whitish stubby forms. A broken crystal may show a typical dark x-like pattern. It is a tough brittle mineral with a hardness between 4 and 7. A variety of andalusite known as *chiastolite* is found in some slates. When the crystals are broken across they may show a cross-shaped pattern caused by impurities enclosed in the silicate crystals during their formation. Andalusite occurs in contact aureoles found in clayey rocks, in muscovite schists and other rocks, and in pegmatites.

Sillimanite is another hard aluminium silicate and occurs usually in white, compact, fibrous or needle-shaped crystals or aggregates. It occurs in the inner parts of metamorphic aureoles where the highest temperatures acted upon clayey rocks. It also occurs in regionally metamorphosed rocks that reached high temperatures.

Kyanite (aluminium silicate) occurs as dark blue bladed crystal aggregates or, rarely, single perfect crystals. It is a brittle mineral, cleaved in two directions, one conspicuous and one faint, and it breaks easily in a third direction. Kyanite has the strange property of having hardness 4.5 in one direction and 6.5 to 7 at right angles to this. It has a vitreous to pearly lustre.

Staurolite is an unusual mineral in being composed of alternate layers of kyanite and iron hydroxide. The common crystal form is an orthorhombic prism, but this mineral may occur in one or another of two twinned forms as on p. 113. It is an iron aluminium silicate in which the oxygen-silicon tetrahedra occur individually, and some magnesium and manganese are usually present. In colour staurolite is mostly a reddish or yellowish brown, but it may be almost black.

Each of these metamorphic minerals has another special significance. It characterizes a degree or grade of metamorphism, from slight in the case of chlorite to intense where sillimanite occurs. These *guide* or *index minerals,* as they might be called, occur in a definite order found in many parts of the world where the original rocks had a suitable composition to allow them to form.

Regional metamorphism

As the name suggests, this kind of metamorphism is developed over wide areas, involving thousands of square kilometres of rock thousands of metres thick. Such changes as we imagine occurring to give this kind of metamorphism must have been produced by some major event in the crust. One is left in no doubt that high temperatures and great pressures have been involved, and these together mean burial deep below the surface. When we look at the way in which these rocks are distributed across the face of the earth two things strike us. Metamorphic rocks occupy virtually all the areas of the great Precambrian continental shields and they also occur in parts of old fold mountain ranges. In both cases thousands of metres of rock have been eroded away from above the metamorphic formations now on view. These crystalline rocks are in many places found together with great masses of granite and other coarse-grained igneous rocks. This, too, shows that they were once very deeply buried and hot.

In regionally metamorphosed rocks the many new minerals that have been formed are different from those in a contact aureole. Some of them are found only in these rocks and in no others. Most of them are important silicates such as chlorite, epidote, biotite, garnet, staurolite, kyanite and sillimanite.

Chlorite is a greenish mineral, mostly occurring in small green scales and plates. It has a sheet structure of ions and includes iron, magnesium and aluminium; so in some ways it is rather like mica. It is a soft mineral sometimes occurring as clusters of tiny crystals in cavities, but usually it is scattered as minute scales throughout the rock.

Epidote is another green mineral containing iron and aluminium, and calcium is a further element in its composition. The silicon-oxygen tetrahedra in this mineral are in pairs which are not further bonded to one another. Coarsely crystalline, granular epidote is rather scarce, but it is this mineral which commonly colours green the veins, joints and similar surfaces in rocks.

Garnets are interesting silicate minerals; the name covers a whole family of iron, manganese, calcium, aluminium, magnesium or chromium-containing substances. They all have a distinctive 12- or 24-sided crystal form and many have beautiful colours. Indeed, their fine crystal shapes (cubic system) and rich colours have elevated some garnets to the rank of semi-precious stones. It is very difficult to distinguish one kind of garnet from another without optical or chemical analysis.

REGIONAL METAMORPHIC ROCKS

Heat and pressure have affected the formation of all the new minerals and characteristics in metamorphic rocks. As one may expect, in metamorphism on a regional scale the rocks vary greatly in appearance, composition and texture. The heat and pressure involved deform some old minerals and lead to the crystallization of new ones. The newcomers have in most cases either a platey or flaky habit or are lath- or needle-shaped. They tend to be arranged in thin parallel layers, giving the rock a property called *foliation, schistosity* or *banding*. Some rocks undergoing regional metamorphism stubbornly do not become foliated but (usually because of their composition) retain a *granular* texture, rather like lump sugar, or a *dense* texture with grains too small to be seen by the unaided eye.

Rock with a foliated or similar texture show *rock* cleavage (sometimes called *parting*). This is the property of breaking along parallel planes, rather as minerals with a cleavage break along parallel surfaces. There are three kinds of rock cleavage:

Slaty cleavage occurs in fine-grained rocks in which the cleavage may follow planes only microscopic distances apart. It cuts across bedding and other features in the rocks and it may retain the same orientation over wide areas. Under the microscope the tiny mineral grains are seen to have become reorientated so that their largest surfaces all align in one direction, that is, perpendicular to the direction from which the squeeze came. This process can be demonstrated in an experimental way by squeezing a soft material like clay in which is embedded flaky or flat particles or fragments.

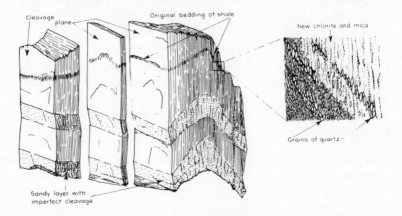

Slaty cleavage occurs best in fine-grained rocks where new chlorite and mica flat crystals may grow. These new minerals align perpendicular to the pressure but quartz grains merely become slightly flattened. In true slates the cleavage may be more conspicuous than the original bedding planes.

Phyllitic parting produces fragments rather thicker than in slates and the cleavage planes tend to be less smooth. Looking closely, one can see tiny glistening specks of chlorite or other minerals on the cleavage surfaces. Indeed, the chlorite is formed from the recrystallization of clay matter under pressure.

Schistose parting is a rougher affair altogether, with rather irregular planes. The individual mineral flakes, however, are all clearly visible, their size and composition depending upon the original nature of the rock and on the intensity of the heating and squeezing it has suffered.

Each of these textures is successively produced by persisting metamorphism. Slaty cleavage is said to be a *low*-grade feature and schistose cleavage a *high*-grade feature. Perhaps the final stage is produced when the minerals in these rocks grow comparatively large and separate into alternating bands. These alternations may each grow to be a few millimetres or centimetres thick, some light in colour, others dark. The rock possessing this texture is called a *gneiss*. As discussed below, the gneisses make up a large family of metamorphic rocks. Some gneisses have splendid rock cleavage or foliation; others tend to be granular.

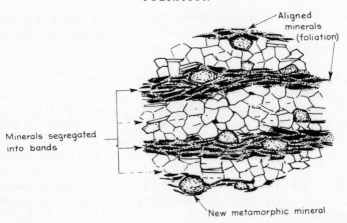

Under great pressure minerals are flattened or recrystallized in flatter forms or newly arise in response to the stress. Commonly they respond to continuing high pressure by becoming segregated into bands, a feature known as *foliation*. Here the rock is magnified 25 times.

THE METAMORPHIC FAMILIES

That there are so many different kinds of metamorphic rocks is really no wonder. Metamorphic rocks may be derived from sedimentary or igneous rocks, and different kinds of metamorphism can affect the same basic materials to produce different results. Most of these rocks are named from their texture and, sometimes, also from their composition – chlorite schist, garnet gneiss, and so on. Here are a few of the commonest types, beginning with the lowest on the grade.

Slate is a fine-grained rock which may have a regular or perfect slaty cleavage. It may be of almost any colour from black to red, green, blue, or even almost white. While its composition depends upon that of the original fine-grained rock, the predominant minerals are mica and chlorite, both platey or flaky minerals, all of which present their larger crystal faces perpendicular to the direction of pressure. Thus at an outcrop of slate one can broadly determine the 'direction of squeeze' which has affected the rock. In this way the slaty cleavage can be a very useful clue to the structure of the region in which it occurs.

As with most rocks that have suffered even a little recrystallization, slate is a very compact non-porous material. Because of its impermeable character and its regular cleavage many slates have been quarried for centuries. From Cornwall, North Wales and the north of England, many a famous slate quarry has yielded material for roofs and other building purposes.

Phyllite is, as we saw above, a metamorphic rock much the same in composition as slate but with mineral grains a little larger. A silky lustre or sheen is found on freshly broken surfaces, but it is lost with prolonged exposure to the air and moisture. In phyllites, as in their lower grade cousins the slates, the flaky minerals are mica and chlorite, but there may be small clots or patches of other, metamorphic, minerals here and there. Tourmaline and garnet are not uncommon in some phyllites. The minerals so characteristic of phyllites can be produced from a slate merely by heating the rock to about 300°C in a strongly sealed container.

Phyllites are not much in demand as building stones – or indeed for any other purpose, which is a pity because there are so many phyllites spread around the world.

Schist is the most typical regional metamorphic rock: it is certainly the most abundant and the schist family is very large. Its parent material may be igneous, sedimentary or low-grade metamorphic rocks, but we commonly think of schists as arising from changes wrought on clay or shaly formations. The mark of all schists is the way in which the thin bands of flaky minerals – mica, chlorite, talc or even haematite – predominate. There may be fine bands of quartz and other granular minerals, but lath-like, fibrous or needle-shaped crystals such as feldspar or hornblende may also be very common. Many a schist has a bright green colour because of the presence of hornblende, chlorite or epidote. Yellow schists may be coloured by mica.

Many of these rocks are attractive to look at, their cleavage surfaces reflect the light and their banded appearance is often pleasing. Nevertheless, the cleavage or parting may render the material rather treacherous for building purposes, and schist is not a popular stone.

Schists are common in many parts of the highlands of Scotland and in parts of Ireland where they may be the deformed and reconstituted equivalents of some of the sedimentary rocks found in Wales and the southern uplands of Scotland. Schists are also found in Anglesey and south-western England.

Amphibolite is a schist-like rock, the bulk of which consists of hornblende and plagioclase crystals. The long thin crystals of these minerals

PLATE 15. *Above left,* light-coloured rather calcareous shale with traces of shelly fossils, Jurassic. Somerset. *Right,* dark shale containing fine particles of carbonaceous matter and iron pyrites, Coal Measures. South Wales. *Below,* cliffs of marl or calcareous clay. Stonebarrow Hill, Charmouth, Dorset.

PLATE 16. *Above,* cliffs of alternating thin bands of Jurassic shale and limestone. Kimmeridge, Dorset. *Below,* cliff of massive marl or siltstone suffering gully erosion. Near Sidmouth, Devon.

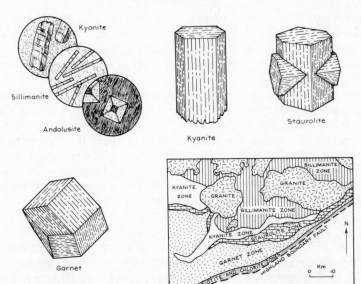

Kyanite

Sillimanite

Andalusite

Kyanite

Staurolite

Garnet

Metamorphic zones associated with great earth movements in what is now part of the Scottish Highlands. The rocks are all essentially of the same chemical composition but the increasing pressure and temperature create the different mineral assemblages, characterized by biotite schists where pressures were relatively low or kyanite and sillimanite schists where they were high. *Upper left*, kyanite, sillimanite and andalusite are seen as typical microscopic crystals, magnification 10 times. Staurolite may be twinned in the form of a cross up to 5–6 cms in height.

give the rock its distinctive *lineation*, like the 'grain' in wood. Amphibolites are green, grey or black colour, weathering pale green, brown or yellow as the ferromagnesian minerals are decomposed. Some green

Where metamorphism acts upon rocks of certain composition, needle- or lath-shaped new crystals such as tourmaline may appear. They tend to grow with their long axes aligned to give a 'grain' to the rock, known as *lineation*.

R.

H

schists and amphibolites contain a green type of augite, biotite and garnet. Medium- to high-grade metamorphism of ferromagnesian igneous rocks, such as basalts, is largely responsible for the amphibolites; some impure calcareous rocks also give rise to amphibolites.

Gneiss is a metamorphic rock easily recognized because of its coarse grain and banded appearance. There is a lesser tendency to split along the bands in gneiss than in schist, and the rock breaks into blocky fragments rather than flat plates or flakes. Only in the highest grades of metamorphism are the gneisses formed, as might be expected from their complete and coarse recrystallization. All kinds of rocks can be 'cooked' in nature to produce gneisses. From igneous rock such as granite or basalt gneisses may arise with quartz and feldspar layers alternating with the different kinds of ferromagnesians. Streaky rocks of this kind are to be found in parts of northern Scotland and many regions of Scandinavia. We are not certain exactly when they were so thoroughly metamorphosed, but radiometric dating of some of the local rock suggests that they are among the oldest in Europe, about 2000 million years old.

Gneisses formed from the metamorphism of clayey sedimentary rocks such as greywackes possess a similarly banded aspect, but the layers of quartz and feldspar alternate with bands of flaky or fibrous minerals such as mica, hornblende, kyanite, staurolite and sillimanite. Graphite occurs in layers in some gneisses in various parts of the world.

Marble is one of the metamorphic rocks valued by architects and sculptors and most people are familiar with it. Essentially it is composed of calcite or dolomite derived from the metamorphism of limestones. In marble the mineral grains are larger than in the original sedimentary rock, perhaps having been completely recrystallized. Fossils which may have been present in the original rock are in most cases deformed or completely obliterated. Marble does not show rock cleavage, but the crystals of calcite may be generally aligned in the same direction in response to the metamorphic pressure. Foliation cannot be seen in most pure marbles because the grains are all the same colour.

In its purest form marble is snowy white and may look like cake icing sugar. Nevertheless there are many beautifully tinted or mottled marbles, the colours resulting from small impurities that were in the original rock. From tiny amounts of the iron oxide, haematite, come red hues; from the iron hydroxide, limonite, come brown and yellow tints; green colours are produced by diopside, hornblende, talc or

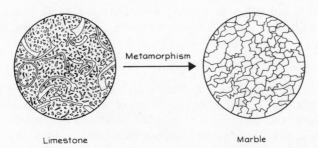

Limestone Marble

A limestone containing shell fragments set in fine-grained calcium carbonate is by metamorphism turned into marble, a rock in which the grains are of interlocking calcite crystals. Magnified 10 times. (After Laporte).

serpentine. Black marbles contain tiny grains of bituminous matter.

Some of the best marbles quarried in Britain came from the Torquay area of south Devon at the end of the nineteenth century. Here a low-grade regional metamorphism has recrystallized the fossiliferous lime-stones, and the patterns of the coral skeletons and shells within have made several varieties of stone that were very popular with the Victorians.

Quartzites are quartz rocks, some of which are made by the meta-morphism of a pure or quartz-rich sandstone. *Metaquartzites* is the name given to quartzites produced by metamorphism: *orthoquartzites* are sandstones with a quartz cement deposited from water in the pore spaces. It is not always easy to distinguish quartzite from some sand-stones because it rarely takes on any foliation. Quartzites lack pore spaces and may have lost any fossils the original sandstone had. Under the hammer quartzites break into sharp-edged fragments, but a hefty blow may be needed because the rock breaks right through the quartz grains rather than round them.

Quartzites can form under any kind of metamorphism and even under 'non-metamorphic conditions' at shallow depths where no other metamorphism is going on.

Like marbles, the purest quartzites are white, but the same im-purities may produce the same colour variations. Many of the original minor constituents of the sandstone, such as feldspar, mica, tourmaline, garnet and zircon, may survive.

Some fine metaquartzites occur among the metamorphic rocks of Scotland, and orthoquartzites are present in the Cambrian strata of the

Midlands and Welsh Borderland, and North and South Wales. A few have been used for road stone or building, others for glass making.

A METAMORPHIC ROCK ARRAY

The varied processes of metamorphism can produce a bewildering array of rocks. Trying to find some sort of order or pattern in the way in which the regional metamorphic rocks occur, geologists have distinguished the metamorphic zones mentioned on page 113. Within these zones we see the production of new minerals which can, we think, only take place between certain temperatures and pressures. There seem to be three common associations of metamorphic rocks in these zones, each one representing part of the crust where a particular temperature range and other conditions prevailed.

Each association is named after a common rock (or mineral) in it.

1. GREENSCHIST ASSOCIATION.   temperatures 150°C–250°C, low grades of metamorphism.

2. EPIDOTE-AMPHIBOLITE ASSOCIATION.   temperatures 250°C–450°C, medium-grade metamorphism.

3. AMPHIBOLITE ASSOCIATION.   temperatures 450°C–700°C, high-grade metamorphism.

For example:

CALCAREOUS SHALE (containing Na, Ca, Fe, Mg, Al, Si, O).

Temperature rises to 200°C

Albite
Chlorite } are formed
Epidote

= GREENSCHIST

Temperature rises to 600°C

various plagioclase
feldspars
hornblende } are formed
quartz

= AMPHIBOLITE

PLATE 17. Limestones. *Above left,* fossiliferous Silurian limestone from Dudley, ×0.25 approx.; *right,* limestone with crinoid columnals, Carboniferous of Derbyshire, ×0.5 approx. *Centre left,* limestone made largely of freshwater snail shells, Jurassic of Dorset, ×0.25 approx.; *right,* pisolitic limestone, Jurassic of Gloucestershire, ×0.5 approx. *Below left,* polished sections of oolitic limestone, Jurassic of Oxfordshire, ×0.5 approx.; *right,* micrograph of ooliths in oolitic limestone, Jurassic of Gloucestershire, ×25.0 approx.

PLATE 18. Limestone terrain. *Above left,* carboniferous Limestone escarpment. Eglwyseg Mountain, N. Wales. *Right,* cliffs and stacks of chalk. Old Harry Rocks, Dorset. *Below left,* solution-weathered surface of limestone forming 'grikes'. Bigrigg, Cumbria. *Right,* stalactitic deposits of calcium carbonate in Swildon's Hole. Mendip Hills.

One of the puzzling things about the progressive regional metamorphism of rocks is that many of the ultimate products seem to
resemble granite in their composition and appearance. Traced across
country, some metamorphic rocks become interlayered with bands of
granite and a distinctive mixture of the two results. It is called a
migmatite – a mixed rock of schist (or gneiss) and granite. In their turn
the migmatites seem to grade into 'granity' rocks with large abundant
feldspar crystals and shadowy remnants of the schistose or layered
structure. A little farther on the whole formation resembles granite in

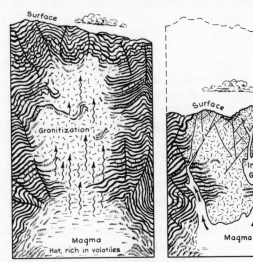

The extreme form of metamorphism is where the original rock becomes
completely reorganized and in effect melted under great pressure and heat.
It may crystallize into something like granite or it may become assimilated
into true granite magma and behave as an intrusive mass. (After Fagan).

every way. One explanation of all this is that the granite is the result of
extreme metamorphism and that the other rocks are steps in the
changing of sedimentary rocks into granite. It is a very different idea
of the origin of granite from that which holds the rock to have been
produced from a magma. It is called *granitization*. The granitization
theory enthusiasts have a little motto which summarizes the idea –
Per migma ad magma. This means 'By mixing to (make) magma' and
it is a good way to explain how many granites have been formed.

CHAPTER 8

THE LIVING DEAD: FOSSILS

MANY a museum has a display of fossils; fossils turn up in junk shops and occasionally they are found decorating a mantelpiece or a desk-top. There is even a vogue for mounting some of them as 'modern art'. Perhaps fossils hold a special fascination because they are the remains of things long since dead, dead maybe for hundreds of millions of years. The word 'fossil' is used these days not only to identify a part of an animal or plant that has been preserved in a deposit, but also to indicate any trace of the activity of organisms. *Trace fossils*, as the latter kind are called, may be footprints, trails, burrows, and even nests and feeding marks.

The incredibly large number of different fossils now recognized is thought to represent not more than a small fraction of the kinds of organisms that have lived on earth. We shall never know what the exact number has been. At this point a word is necessary about how living things – and fossils – are named. The system in use today was invented by the Swedish naturalist Carl Linnaeus about two hundred years ago. He arranged the known animals (and plants) into groups on the basis of their similarities. The groups in turn were placed in larger categories, and these in larger still, each category having a number of character-istics shared by all its members. In this classification biologists have attempted to record the 'family tree' relationships of different living things. For example, our household pets *Canis familiaris* and *Felis domesticus* are awarded Linnean names as in the figure.

As one might expect, fossils are named on much the same basis; not all scientists are agreed on how precisely it should be done.

There must be about a million species of organisms in the world today, and this figure reflects the fact that life is more diverse and successful than ever before.

About one-sixth of all modern species of animals live in the sea, and half of these live on the sandy or muddy sea floor. About half of the latter possess some hard part or parts which may survive after the animal dies. Such hard parts may become enclosed in sediment and preserved as fossils. On the face of it, then, less than 15% of all living marine species may become fossil and hence be regarded as a sample

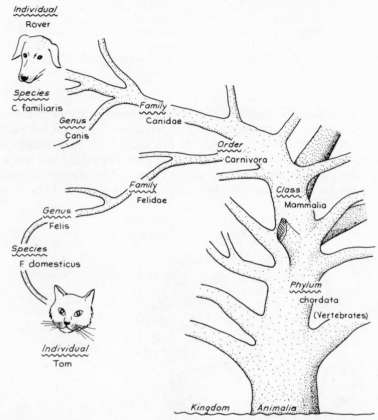

The Linnean system of names applied to household animals, the dog *Canis familiaris* and the cat *Felis domesticus*. Fossils are treated in the same way as far as possible.

comparable with ancient faunas. Although the number is increasing each year, we only know rather less than 150,000 species of fossils as yet. (The proportion of fossil plants known is even smaller.) Most of these are of creatures that had hard parts made of calcium carbonate, or calcium phosphate, or silica or chitin, shells, teeth, bones, and the like. Soft tissues are hardly ever fossilized.

The numbers of modern species most susceptible to fossilization, having some hard resistant tissues, are:

Invertebrates	170,000
Vertebrates	49,000
Plants	350,000
A total of	569,000 preservable species

The number of individuals in any species is commonly very great and, in spite of the low probabilities of preservation, fossils are not really uncommon. In many fossil species the individuals are fantastically abundant. From various pieces of evidence we judge that fossil species lasted on average up to twelve million years, and the number of plant and animal species that may be preserved in the rocks could be more

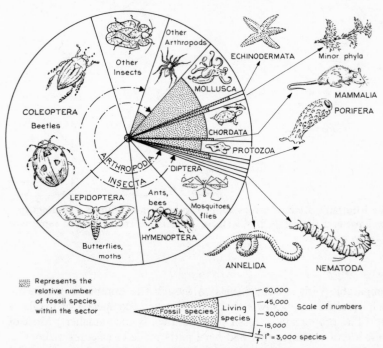

Numbers of fossil and living organisms. The number of previously unknown living animals and plants is rising today relatively slowly. New species of fossil animals and plants are being described in great numbers each year. (After Miller and Campbell).

than ten million. There is a lot of work ahead before we know more than a very few of them.

When we examine all the different kinds of fossils together in any one rock we see that many are preserved where the organisms lived and died. Others have been moved from where they lived to a new site for burial – which is one of the reasons why fossil clams are so common and why fossil birds are so rare. The fossil record is not a random sample of past life but is a rather selected sample of organisms that lived in or near a place where sediments were accumulating. Again,

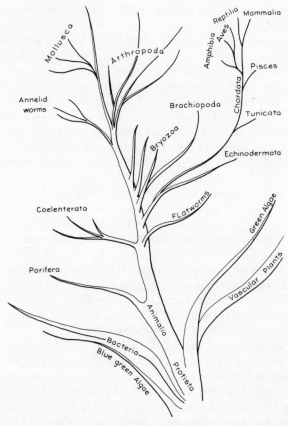

A suggested 'family tree' for some of the major groups of living organisms. Not all groups are equally well represented as fossils, see opposite.

this is one of the reasons why sea creatures are common fossils and upland or desert animals such as giraffes or ostriches are not.

FOSSILIZATION

So far we have seen that fossils resemble, to a greater or lesser degree, modern animals and plants. They occur only in sedimentary rocks or, in rare cases, in volcanic rocks. Only very exceptionally are fossils preserved which are the almost unaltered remains of an animal or plant. The frozen mammoths found in the frozen bogs of Siberia are perhaps the most striking examples. They were small hairy elephants living in the forests of the Ice Age. Although they are now extinct, we know a great deal about them.

Altered remains are much more common and much less spectacular. Nevertheless many cases are known of the most delicate structures and even colours being preserved intact. The vast majority of fossils, however, have undergone some alteration since the death of the organism. Perhaps the simplest kind of alteration is to a less complex chemical composition by *leaching* away of soluble components.

Distillation is the kind of decomposition in which the oxygen, hydrogen and nitrogen of the organic material have escaped. All that may remain is a black carbonaceous film, as in the case of many plant fossils.

Many cases are known where fossilized shells and bones have been altered by the addition of material from percolating water. In this way the fossils may be seriously harmed, but in some instances the material is preserved in the finest detail. The process is called *permineralization*.

A further step in this process is where the original shell or skeletal matter is dissolved away and another substance takes its place. This we know as *mineralization* or *petrifaction*. Calcite and quartz are the two commonest minerals found replacing fossil tissues; dolomite, pyrite and others also behave in this way. When the original material has all gone the fossil is called a *pseudomorph*.

Moulds or *impressions* are left in any soft mud or sandy material capable of retaining an imprint. The cavity left when a fossil shell falls from the rock is just such a mould or impression. If it were to be filled by a later mineral deposit a *cast* would be formed. Originally hollow shells may be infilled at some stage, and this infilling is sometimes referred to as a *core* or *steinkern*. Most fossiliferous rock formations show several kinds of preservation of the fossils. As often as not, the surface weathering of the rock rather than the early mineralogical

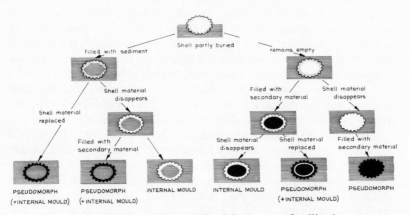

Some ways in which a shell might become fossilized.

changes within it seems to control whether the fossils can be extracted in one form or another. Before it ultimately resides in a collector's bag a fossil may have had a very complicated chemical history, but most fossils never reach such an exalted end. For them it is ashes to ashes and dust to dust in the rock cycle.

LIFE BEFORE FOSSILS

If we search back far enough into the geological past we find that rocks older than about six hundred million years lack fossils, except in a very few rare cases. The earliest Cambrian fossils are quite complicated, and even such Precambrian traces of life as are imprinted upon the rocks are by no means the most primitive that we can imagine. From nearly every continent there are Precambrian fossils that resemble lowly marine invertebrates. A few of the most ancient fossils, however, are like nothing we know today.

The instances where Precambrian organisms did become fossilized indicate unusual circumstances. For example, in the Gunflint chert of Ontario, Canada, a remarkable range of primitive plants – microscopic algae, fungi and bacteria – has been preserved in very fine silica. Just how this came about we do not know.

But the search for the earliest forms of life in the rocks, and indeed for the origin of life itself, is not confined merely to looking for fossils in the usual sense of the word. Even the simplest organisms of the present are made of protoplasm, and what versatile stuff protoplasm is. It is not surprising that on analysis it is found to consist of very complex molecules containing carbon, hydrogen, oxygen and a host of other elements. Life is based on the chemistry of carbon, and when the temperatures or pressures range outside the fairly close-set limits for the necessary reactions to take place, life cannot exist. For the most part, we can say that where there is water life is possible; it is a substance essential for the chemical activity of living things.

This bit of knowledge helps narrow down the period of time and the range of conditions of rock formation in which life – and hence, fossils – could have existed. Until the earth had cooled to something like its present state life could not exist. The oldest rocks to show signs of the existence of water may possibly still contain clues about the earliest forms of life.

When an electric spark is caused in a mixture of water vapour, methane gas and other gases which can occur naturally in the atmosphere, some of the molecules begin to link up into more complex arrangements. They produce what are called amino-acids, and amino-acids are the simplest carbon compounds which are built into the molecules essential to protoplasm. This could have happened during electric storms long ago. If enough of these little chemical building blocks were eventually present in the early earth atmosphere and sea, sooner or later some would link into more permanent arrangements which might develop the ability to capture carbon compounds from round about and so increase their own size and composition. It sounds simple, but it must have been a very slow and enormously complicated process of evolution. Hundreds of millions of years may have been needed even after the right geological conditions prevailed.

In those days the atmosphere was mostly carbon dioxide, not nitrogen and oxygen, and the earth was exposed to the intense ultraviolet radiation from the sun. Perhaps only in the deeper waters of the sea could the complex chemical systems survive which had the ability to grow in a regular way – to reproduce themselves. So far and so much is chemistry. The next steps to produce a living cell from such chemical activity are still far from understood. There may have been many complex arrangements of carbon-containing molecules which did not survive, but at last a carbon-bearing system which enclosed itself in a little bag or membrane was evolved. It proved more successful than any previous construction of molecules for within the enclosed space chemical activity could continue with less risk of losing the ions or molecular bits and pieces it required. Foreign, useless or harmful

PLATE 19. Cleavage in non-clayey rocks, such as these sandstones (*above*) at Crinan, Argyll, and these limestones (*below*) at Torquay, may be conspicuous despite rock folding and other features. Only very fine-grained rocks may be cleaved to give slates.

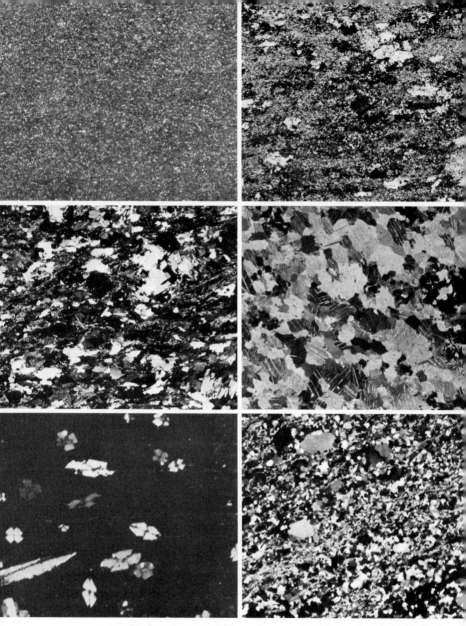

PLATE 20. Various metamorphic rocks seen in thin section by polarised light. *Top left,* slate, a mass of tiny flakes of chlorite, sericite and quartz; *right,* quartz-biotite schist with somewhat darker streaks where the biotite is more common; *centre left,* sillimanite-garnet-mica schist produced by thermal alteration of a shale; *right,* green diopside-garnet marble resulting from the alteration of an impure limestone; *below left,* a thermally metamorphosed slate with chiastolite crystals; *right,* thermally altered slate with andalusite and cordierite crystals. Magnification approx. ×35.

chemicals could be excluded. The cell, the essential building brick of organic tissues and the simplest truly living thing, had arrived. It used chemical energy to build more carbon-containing molecules into its structure but it could only survive if a limited range of chemical and physical conditions existed.

To supplement the 'purely chemical' sources of energy early living matter may have derived some of its strength from an ability to use the energy of sunshine. Plants do this with great success in a process called photosynthesis, turning carbon dioxide and water into sugars by this means. Way back in the Precambrian eon some cells developed such an ability. The particular compound which takes care of this function is called chlorophyll. It is green, indispensable, and has become the molecular trademark of many plant cells. Animals do not have it.

How life became divided into animals and plants is not certain, but the early organisms which gave rise to animals were those which had not the ability to use chlorophyll. They raided or ate the local organisms that had, and found the arrangement was adequate. So some groups existed on water, carbon dioxide, a few (nutrient) salts and sunlight; others, unable to survive on such fare, engulfed and used the chemistry of cells that already had the necessary protoplasmic composition.

So far so good, and every cell for himself, it might be said, was the rule for these early Precambrian organisms. At length a new mode of life was adopted by some cells which found that by sticking (literally) close together they all benefited. Until then only a unicellular mode of life existed; multicellular organisms came at the point when there was an advantage in such a link-up.

The next stage in the sequence leading to the range of animals and plants seen in most Precambrian fossiliferous rocks was that some groups of cells began to perform special tasks for the multicellular colony. These cells all had the same structure, forming a *tissue,* and were supported in their activities by other groups of cells which took on different and complementary tasks. By such division of function the entire colony profited. Both animals and plants had successfully made the breakthrough into multicellular organization long before the dawn of Cambrian time.

Later events which affected the evolution of life on earth have been less difficult to reconstruct or understand. By Cambrian time some animals had the ability to secrete hard skeletal parts. In Ordovician times they began to use calcium carbonate in skeletal tissues on an unprecedented scale. New-found abilities like these (there were others) may have been dependent upon an overall progressive change in the earth's atmosphere by which more and more free oxygen had become available (see page 125). In the shallow seas shell-bearing and other calcareous creatures were building new environments – shell banks, coral reefs and colonies – which offered opportunity of food and shelter to many other new forms of life. All the phyla of modern animals had appeared before the Ordovician period was over.

From the sea to fresh water and from water to land were transitions various animals and plants made by Devonian time. Freely available oxygen in the atmosphere enabled a faster production of energy to be made by animals and the development of food and water-conducting tissues in plants helped them colonize the wet landscapes of the day. Rapid evolution followed; ultimately the earth was thoroughly invested with living things.

MOLECULAR PALAEONTOLOGY

The word 'fossil' will perhaps conjure in one's mind the image of a shell, or a bone or a leaf. These are the common fossils which we may collect on a country ramble or along the sea-shore. In recent years, however, another kind of fossil has been collected and studied. It is the (fossil) organic compound which is trapped in sediment when organic matter is buried. As such, of course, it is not a solid hard object that can be hacked out of the rock with a hammer. If we examine the geological role of plankton, the miriad floating organisms in the sea, we see that it provides a constant rain of organic matter falling to the sea floor. As the sediments themselves are compressed over the ages, so this this organic material is converted into oil in sedimentary rocks. The oil is a mixture of carbon compounds derived from once living things. The carbon compounds may include substances unaltered from what they were when forming part of a living organism. They are, in fact, traces of past life and hence are fossils.

Molecular palaeontology is the study of such fossil organic compounds, derived from once-living things. The surprising thing is that most sedimentary rocks have some traces of the incredible numbers of organic compounds that are involved in the chemistry of life. When living things die, their substances tend to disperse, and many of the more complex ones are broken down by bacteria. Others combine with oxygen or water, but a few are hardy enough to keep their distinctive molecular structure intact long after the animal or plant of which they once formed a part has completely disappeared. They may survive as particles within the pore spaces in sedimentary rocks, coating the mineral grains, or lying in solution in the pore-waters. Tiny as the amounts of such organic compounds may be, we have now the means of extracting, analysing and identifying many of them.

Many of those organic compounds essential to protoplasm and known as *amino-acids* thus survive decomposition of their parent material and only slowly break down in the rocks. Some survive for many millions of years and a few are known from ancient Precambrian sediments. Knowing how long it may take for some amino-acids and other organic 'geochemicals' to decompose, we may one day be able to use them as a sort of 'geological clock' much as we use radioactive decay to measure the age of certain rocks.

FOSSILS AND TIME

From simple beginnings millions of years ago to the immense variety of living things today there has been an unbroken process of change. We call it evolution. As conditions on earth have altered, so life has modified its many forms in attempts to strike the right balance and survive. Not all living things have been successful in this; many have

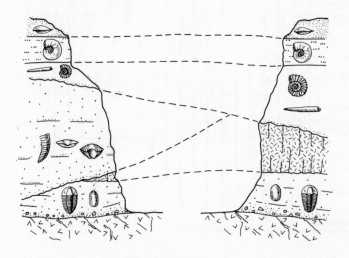

Correlation, or matching, of separated outcrops of once continuous beds of rock can be made by recognizing the fossils these beds contain. In this way complicated geological histories can be discovered.

failed and become extinct. Imprisoned in the rocks are the fossils which tell the story; layer upon layer of sedimentary rock take us from one moment of geological time to another. As each sediment was deposited the life of the time left its remnants as fossils.

Wherever we find strata exposed in depth we normally expect to find the first formed, the oldest of them, at the bottom and the youngest at the top. William Smith, a civil engineer, put forward nearly two hundred years ago the idea that the order of the strata in a section gave an order to the distribution of fossils there; the oldest at the bottom and the youngest at the top. It was no great step to deduce that each assemblage of fossils may be unique to that particular time of rock

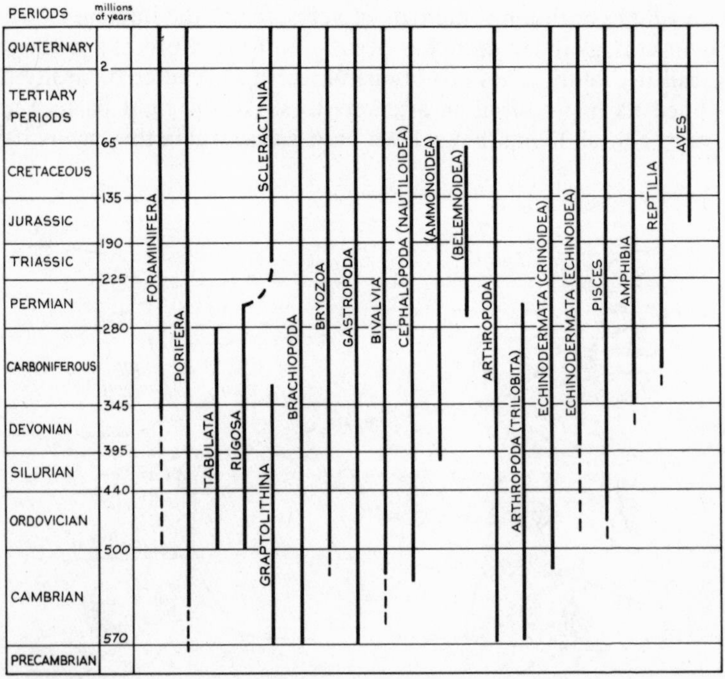

PERIODS	millions of years
QUATERNARY	2
TERTIARY PERIODS	65
CRETACEOUS	135
JURASSIC	190
TRIASSIC	225
PERMIAN	280
CARBONIFEROUS	345
DEVONIAN	395
SILURIAN	440
ORDOVICIAN	500
CAMBRIAN	570
PRECAMBRIAN	

Column labels: FORAMINIFERA, PORIFERA, SCLERACTINIA, TABULATA, RUGOSA, GRAPTOLITHINA, BRACHIOPODA, BRYOZOA, GASTROPODA, BIVALVIA, CEPHALOPODA (NAUTILOIDEA), (AMMONOIDEA), (BELEMNOIDEA), ARTHROPODA, ARTHROPODA (TRILOBITA), ECHINODERMATA (CRINOIDEA), ECHINODERMATA (ECHINOIDEA), PISCES, AMPHIBIA, REPTILIA, AVES

Fossils can be used to identify the particular geological period in which the rock containing them was formed. The geological ranges of most of the major animal groups extend back, however, a mere 500–600 million years.

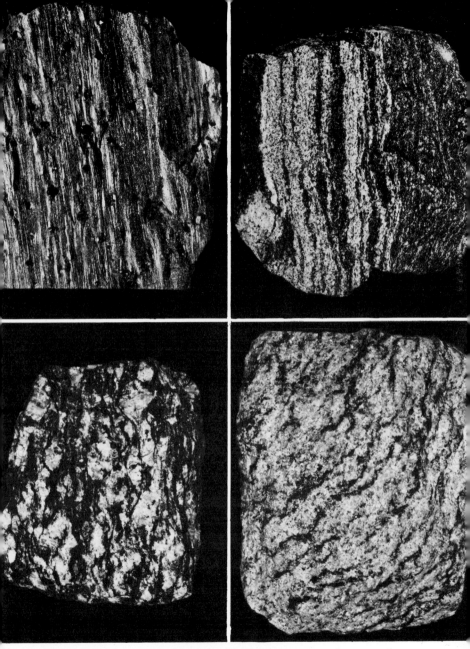

PLATE 21. Scottish metamorphic rocks. *Top left*, garnet crystals scattered in a ground mass of quartz-chlorite schist; *right*, strongly banded schist, dark layers of hornblende crystals, lighter streaks of quartz and feldspar; *below left*, coarsely crystalline gneiss with 'augen' or clots of quartz and feldspar in a ground mass of quartz, feldspar and mica; *right*, a highly altered gneiss beginning to lose its banded or foliated texture. (All approx. ×0.25.)

PLATE 22. *Above* cleaved and puckered slate with small veins of quartz. Watergate Bay, Cornwall. *Centre*, sharp recumbent folds in schist. Craig Llwyd, Anglesey. *Below*, gneisses with thin granitic (pale) intrusions between the beds. Kennack Bay, Cornwall.

formation, different from those above and below. Within a few decades enough sections had been examined and sufficient fossils collected to show that between the Precambrian and the present there is an un-broken succession of fossils to mark every moment of geological time. Each span of time has had its own characteristic organisms and has left its own special species of fossils.

By using the various fossils as 'date stamps' or emblems of geological age, geologists are able to *correlate* rocks from one area to another.

Not all forms of life have evolved at the same rate. Some fossils appear briefly in the record and others are to be encountered through great thicknesses of rock. The fossils most useful to the geologist often are those with the more restricted vertical range – their distri-bution represents a shorter period of time.

Even on the basis of these fossils we cannot say directly how old a rock is in terms of years. We can only say which period it belongs to. For an idea of age in terms of years we must resort to radiometric methods where possible.

FOSSILS AND ENVIRONMENTS

Collecting fossils is, like many things, easier when you know where to go and what to look for. For example, the best fossil sea-urchins may be found in chalky limestones and the best graptolites in glossy black shales. The collector soon recognizes that the distribution of fossils from rock to rock is not a random affair. Certain fossils seem to 'prefer' certain lithologies.

Of course this is not a very scientific way of stating the case. We could say that rock lithology seems to control fossil content. It sounds (and is) more scientific. What, however, can be said about the actual preferences that the organisms of the past had for the places in which they lived? Today we recognize that each species differs in its food, temperature tolerance and other requirements. Its distribution is largely controlled by these things and, in the case of aquatic organisms, by the factors which control the kind of sediment being deposited. Each organism has its *habitat*, the kind of place, or environment, where it lives best. The classification of habitats is usually based on environ-mental factors that seem to be the most important in determining animal distribution.

The most obvious division of habitats is into aquatic and terrestrial.

Aquatic environments may be freshwater, marine or brackish, shallow, deep, rocky, tropical, and so on. Most fossils are the remains of aquatic, indeed marine, organisms so we may reasonably confine ourselves to a view of marine environments as in the figure below. There seems to be no reason for thinking that environments in the ancient seas were very different, if at all, from those in the seas of today.

We distinguish here too different modes of life among the inhabitants of these environments. On the bottom is the *benthos*; floating in

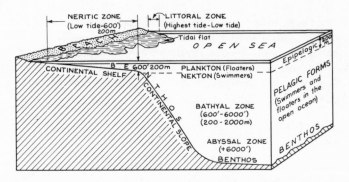

Most of the organisms that may become fossils live in the sea where they may float or swim (*plankton, nekton*) or live on the bottom (*benthos*).

the water is the *plankton*; swimming by is the *nekton*. The benthos may be preserved in place where it dies, but the *pelagic* or free organism may be preserved in place where it dies, but the *pelagic* or free organisms have to fall to the bottom before they can become fossils. Benthonic animals in sandy areas stand a good chance of becoming fossils, but their neighbours in rocky areas or in the open sea above may only rarely become interred and fossilized.

The fossil collector, then, may recognize differences between fossil samples of the same age collected in different localities. He may conclude that they represent differences in the environments in which the living populations existed. Some differences may be due to the hazards of preservation. Part of the fascination in palaeontology lies in the challenge of trying to recognize different assemblages of fossils from place to place and to understand why the groups are distributed in the way they are.

CHAPTER 9

THE IMMORTAL FEW

No book on rocks would be complete without a few words on the various major groups of fossils that are to be found in the common sedimentary rocks. From what was said in the last chapter it will be obvious that most fossils represent organisms once alive in shallow seas, seas that spread and receded over periods of millions of years across the low-lying parts of the continents. Geological events controlled the existence and evolution of these shelf seas and the processes which they represent seem still to be going on today. We know that the continents move, not only up and down in broad warps and narrow mountain chains, but also sideways in the slow but majestic motion we call 'continental drift'. Thus continents have changed their position and shape on the face of the earth, with important consequences for the plants and animals living on them and in the seas along their margins. With continental movement taking place climates change and the inhabitants change and adapt to meet the new conditions. Thus even in the high latitudes today we can find fossils of corals and other creatures that indicate warm or tropical conditions.

The fossils we will outline in this chapter are largely those of the marine invertebrate animals. Many books on fossils seem to resemble catalogues rather than natural histories and this is because there are so many different types of fossils to be found in the record of the rocks. Few experts become very familiar with more than one major group of fossils and the average geologist tends to seek specialist advice about the precise nature of the fossils he finds. Nevertheless the value of being able to recognise the broad categories to which an assemblage of fossil organisms belongs is very real. For the amateur there is always the attraction of finding something new – for we are a long way from cataloguing all the different fossils that have been presented. A splendid account of some of the modern animals in the groups listed below is given in *Life on the Sea Shore*, a companion volume in this series.

FOSSIL ANIMALS

PROTOZOA. Of all the microscopic unicellular organisms to be pre-served in the rocks, the *foraminifera* are among the commonest as fossils. This is because many of them had shells or *tests* of calcareous or other material. These range in size from about six hundredths of a millimetre to about 20 centimetres long. Most are less than 1 mm in diameter. The tests are of many different shapes and patterns. Most foraminifera today live in the oceans but some prefer less salty water and a few like fresh water. They are known with certainty from rocks of Ordovician age onwards, and in some formations they are very abundant.

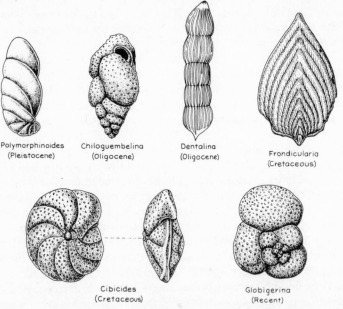

Polymorphinoides
(Pleistocene)

Chiloguembelina
(Oligocene)

Dentalina
(Oligocene)

Frondicularia
(Cretaceous)

Cibicides
(Cretaceous)

Globigerina
(Recent)

Foraminifera. Many of these tiny calcareous shells or *tests* are constituted of several chambers arranged in a wide variety of ways. Magnified × 100.

PORIFERA. The porifera are the sponges, the simplest multicellular animals. They have hard parts made of flexible material but they may also be impregnated with tiny calcareous or siliceous particles (*spicules*). They are primarily marine organisms, living anchored to the sea floor,

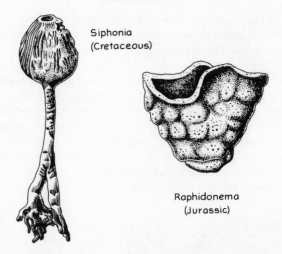

Siphonia
(Cretaceous)

Raphidonema
(Jurassic)

Fossil sponges. Where the fragile sponge skeleton has been preserved more or less intact it may show a characteristic vase- or flower-like shape as in the case of these two sponges from the Mesozoic rocks of Britain. *Siphonia, left*; *Raphidonema, right*. (About half size).

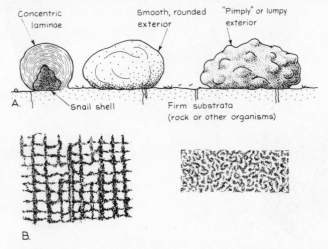

Concentric laminae

Smooth, rounded exterior

"Pimply" or lumpy exterior

A.

Snail shell

Firm substrata (rock or other organisms)

B.

Stromatoporoids (A) are cabbage-shaped or rounded masses of very thin calcium carbonate layers. Some began by attaching to a coral, snail or other shell, later smothering it. Large colonies reach a metre or more across and formed reefs and mounds on the sea floor. Their microstructure (B) is used in identification, but the animal which produced it remains unknown.

and range in size from 1 mm to 2 m in diameter. Many fossil sponges have characteristic bulbous or vase-like shapes. They seem to have been around since late Precambrian time.

COELENTERATA. This group includes many kinds of marine animals, but by far the most important in the fossil world are the corals. Corals are solitary or colonial (with many individuals or *polyps* sharing a site) in habit and live in warm clear seas. Their skeletons are preserved as calcium carbonate structures of great delicacy and, in some cases, much complexity too. The corals of the Palaeozoic era have a clear bilateral symmetry in cross-section, but Mesozoic and Cainozoic corals have a six-fold symmetry.

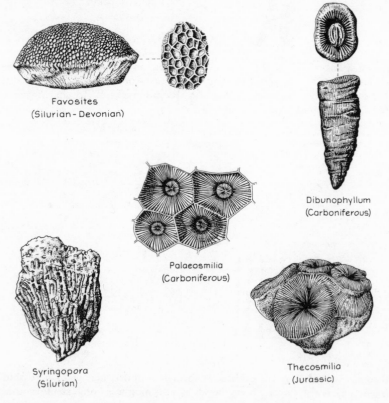

Favosites
(Silurian - Devonian)

Dibunophyllum
(Carboniferous)

Palaeosmilia
(Carboniferous)

Syringopora
(Silurian)

Thecosmilia
(Jurassic)

Fossil corals. Palaeozoic and Mesozoic corals are rather easily recognizable and are usually found in limestones or calcareous shales. (About half size).

Jellyfish also belong to the coelenterata but, lacking hard parts, are very rarely preserved as fossils. Several other calcareous fossils of a problematic nature are also referred to the coelenterata.

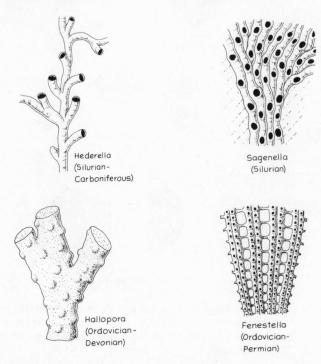

Hederella
(Silurian-
Carboniferous)

Sagenella
(Silurian)

Hallopora
(Ordovician-
Devonian)

Fenestella
(Ordovician-
Permian)

Bryozoa may form encrustations on other objects but their myriad pores and their lace-like patterns are easily distinguished. (After Beerbower). Magnification × 5. These are a few Palaeozoic forms.

BRYOZOA. Microscopic animals living in branched, lattice-like or encrusting colonies are the bryozoa (or polyzoa). The colonies commonly are made from calcium carbonate, have characteristic microstructures, and range from less than 1 cm in diameter to fronds and masses 10 cms or more across. From Ordovician time on they have been common.

BRACHIOPODA. The brachiopods are one of the most numerous and important groups of Palaeozoic fossils. They are bivalve shellfish living on the bottom and may resemble molluscs. Brachiopods are most commonly of the kind with well-made calcareous shells or *valves* but a few

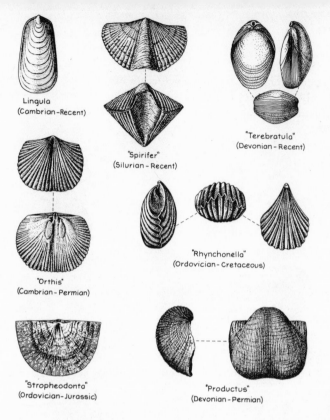

Linqula
(Cambrian-Recent)

"Spirifer"
(Silurian-Recent)

"Terebratula"
(Devonian-Recent)

"Orthis"
(Cambrian-Permian)

"Rhynchonella"
(Ordovician-Cretaceous)

"Stropheodonta"
(Ordovician-Jurassic)

"Productus"
(Devonian-Permian)

Brachiopods are bivalved shellfish in which the shells are bilaterally symmetrical but not mirror images of one another. Here is *Lingula,* the commonest primitive form, and a selection of the most important groups of other brachiopods. (About half size).

primitive kinds have more flimsy chitinous valves. The calcareous or *articulate* (hinged-shelled) brachiopods may have smooth, ribbed or corrugated shells; most are about walnut-size or smaller, a few reach 10 cms across. The brachiopods have progressively declined since Palaeozoic days.

MOLLUSCA. This important phylum includes bivalves (also known as lamellibranchs, pelecypods or clams), snails, chitons and the cephalopods. The last group includes the octopus, pearly nautilus, and squids. There are also the important extinct groups, the rather bullet-like belemnites and the coiled shells known as ammonoids. Molluscs have inhabited freshwaters as well as the seas for a long time and some snails are at home on land. The phylum is known from Cambrian rocks to the

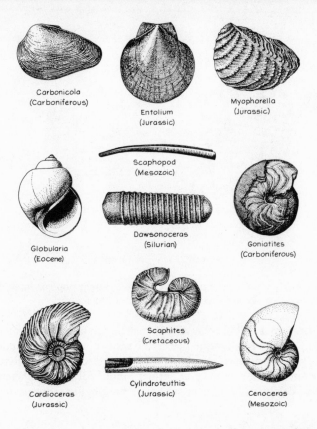

Carbonicola
(Carboniferous)

Entolium
(Jurassic)

Myophorella
(Jurassic)

Scaphopod
(Mesozoic)

Globularia
(Eocene)

Dawsonoceras
(Silurian)

Goniatites
(Carboniferous)

Scaphites
(Cretaceous)

Cardioceras
(Jurassic)

Cylindroteuthis
(Jurassic)

Cenoceras
(Mesozoic)

The mollusc clan is large, varied and successful, including the bivalves, the scaphopods or 'tusk-shells', snails and the once-prolific cephalopods. The last mentioned inhabited straight or coiled, chambered shells but are now reduced to a few marine types such as the nautilus, squid and shell-less octopus. (These figures are about half natural size).

most recent. The belemnites and ammonites are virtually confined to the Mesozoic strata, but some occur in late Palaeozoic rocks.

ARTHROPODA. This highly successful phylum is represented by several groups of fossils, all bearing jointed legs, the characteristic feature. Most arthropods have hard cases or carapaces, which can be preserved as fossils. They seem to inhabit almost every kind of environment and have been present since Precambrian times. Amongst the commonest fossils are trilobites, ostracods, eurypterids and crustaceans (shrimps and the like). Although insects are common enough, they are rare as fossils.

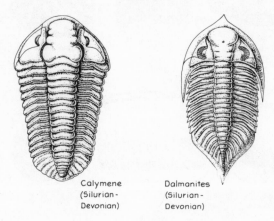

Calymene
(Silurian-
Devonian)

Dalmanites
(Silurian-
Devonian)

The trilobites are some of the fossils that have caught popular imagination. Here are two that are very well known. (About life size).

ECHINODERMATA. This exclusively marine phylum includes animals with spiny skins and a unique five-fold basic symmetry. It includes the many forms of starfish, sea urchins, sea lilies and several other living sea creatures in addition to several extinct kinds. All have a skeleton of crystalline calcite. The first members of the phylum appeared in the

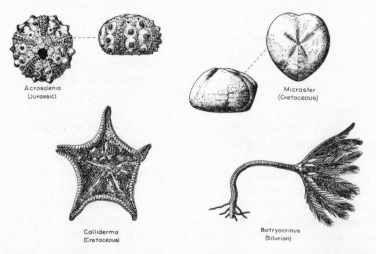

Acrosalenia
(Jurassic)

Microster
(Cretaceous)

Calliderma
(Cretaceous)

Botryocrinus
(Silurian)

Sea urchins, crinoid, and starfish are representatives of the phylum Echinodermata. (About life size).

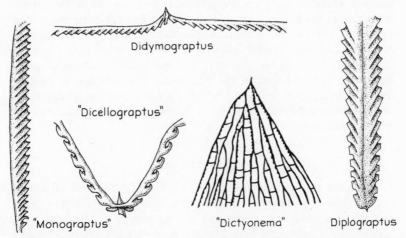

Graptolites are puzzling' fossils in which the fragile skeleton is usually crushed. Broad categories are recognizable by the arrangement of the stipes or 'branches'. (About half natural size).

Cambrian period and there may have been some Precambrian forms. In Palaeozoic times the sea lilies were so numerous that their broken stem parts locally piled up to form crinoidal limestones.

PROTOCHORDATA. A group of animals which is typified today by a few strange little sea-animals, this phylum may include many puzzling fossils. Of these the commonest may be the *graptolites* which were marine planktonic, colonial creatures. The fossils resemble small delicate fronds of plants or bryozoa, but are commonly of a chitinous composition. Most are only a few centimetres across, but the largest may be 2 metres in length. They range in age from the Cambrian to the early Carboniferous, but the majority are found in the Ordovician and Silurian rocks.

CHORDATA. In this phylum are the vertebrate or back-boned animals and a few other less familiar forms. The vertebrates have several kinds of hard parts that may be fossilized – bones, teeth, scales, scutes and bony armour, and much of this material is of a characteristic phosphatic nature. Vertebrate skeletons, however, consist of many bones or parts that tend to fall apart after the death of the animal. Hence complete fossil skeletons are somewhat rare – especially where the animals did not live where sedimentary deposits were forming. Birds are notoriously rare as fossils. The first vertebrate remains are from Ordovician rocks but only in the Devonian did fish become common fossils. Amphibia and then reptiles followed by the close of the early Carboniferous but their heyday was over by the end of Cretaceous time. Mammals appeared first in the Mesozoic. The vertebrates have of course a spectacular geological record with such animals as dinosaurs and other fearsome reptiles in the Mesozoic era and giant mammals in the early Cainozoic.

FOSSIL PLANTS

The number of phyla of plants is rather smaller than that of animal phyla and fossil plants are not generally as numerous as fossil animals. Nevertheless plants are represented by a number of important groups.

Fossil BACTERIA have been found but as they are microscopic and difficult to retrieve we need say nothing about them here. Fossil ALGAE are, however, amongst the commoner plant fossils and some lime-secreting forms have produced the remarkable growths known as STROMATOLITES, preserved in formations from Precambrian to Recent age. *Diatoms*, the microscopic siliceous planktonic single-celled plants, are common in some formations.

BRYOPHYTA include mosses and liverworts and are rare fossils, first occurring in the Carboniferous rocks.

The TRACHEOPHYTA include all the remaining higher plants, club mosses, ferns, seed ferns, ginkos, conifers and flowering plants and mostly occur in non-marine rocks of Carboniferous to Recent age. A few forms are known from rocks as old as Silurian or Ordovician.

There are of course numbers of fossils which have so far defied attempts to put them into one or other of our biological categories. They are for the most part rare and not within the experience of the amateur palaeontologist, but let this not deter the interested collector from putting his 'puzzle-pieces' aside with special care in the hope that something new may be added to our knowledge of the life of the past.

FOSSIL-ROCKS

So numerous are fossils in some rocks that there seems to be more fossil than matrix. Fossils are indeed rock-builders in many instances, perhaps the most obvious being that of coal. On the other hand, such formations as the white Chalk rocks of England and many other places are also made of fossil material, but fossils of quite a different kind are present there. Much of the white chalk limestone is now known to be made up of microscopic algal debris. Of this more anon. These two examples, one black and obvious and the other white but not so obvious, illustrate the point that the skeletal materials of once-living things can and do accumulate locally in sufficient quantity to give rise to rock formations. Apart from plant debris, the commonest material to accumulate so abundantly is calcium carbonate – limestone. Other important 'organic deposits' may consist of silica or phosphate and many of them are commercially valuable.

Let us look at a few instances of the rock forming abilities of some of the organisms we have mentioned. The *protozoa*, in the shape of foraminifera have been so abundant as to produce beds of limestone composed of their remains in two remarkable instances in the past. The earliest of these was in Late Palaeozoic times when the fusulinids, which were tightly rolled many-chambered foraminifera rather like a grain of rice in shape and size, were at their acme in what is now the U.S.A. The second was in early Cainozoic time when the nummulitids, rather penny-sized flat foraminifera, were flourishing in what is now the Middle East. Both groups gave rise to rather handsome limestones, locally in demand as building or ornamental stones. The pyramids of Egypt are at least in part built of nummulitic limestone. Other foraminiferal limestones are much less important and are indeed rare. Today deep sea oozes consisting of the tests of the planktonic *Globigerina* are very slowly accumulating over parts of our ocean floors but in the shallow seas foraminifera do not seem to be as active as at other times in producing calcareous sediments.

The *porifera* rarely have given rise to rock masses but on a few occasions they have been abundant enough to make up local beds wherein all seems to be calcareous sponge debris. Some famous Mesozoic sponge beds occur in southern Britain and western Europe.

The *coelenterata* undoubtedly hold a high place in the rock-building hierarchy in the persons of the stony corals and a fossil group known as stromatoporoids. The very earliest reef-like masses of coral-like organisms, the archaeocyathids, occur in Cambrian rocks but only in the Ordovician do true coral reefs first appear. Palaeozoic coral reefs flourished in all the later periods, some were of immense size and clearly lasted for millions of years, supporting, as do modern coral reefs, all manner of other sea creatures within them and upon their growing surfaces. Triassic reefs are virtually unknown but later Mesozoic and Cainozoic reefs and coralline rocks are common on almost every continent, and they are of great interest from both palaeontological and palaeogeographical viewpoints.

The *bryozoa* are mere shadows of the coelenterata at rock building, but a few forms in Palaeozoic and Mesozoic seas did make domed structures which must have been rather like small coral reefs.

The *brachiopods* may well have lived in great abundance and closely packed on certain Palaeozoic and Mesozoic sea floors but true brachiopod limestones are rather few. Some large Palaeozoic brachiopods lived together in what may have looked like oyster-beds but most other instances of brachiopod-crowded limestones seem to be collections of dead individuals swept together by tides or currents.

Molluscs have produced many beds of limestone in the past, either as oyster or other clam beds, as collections of freshwater snail shells or as the current-sweepings of cephalopods in shallow reaches of the Mesozoic seas. True oyster beds are well known from Mesozoic rocks in many parts of the world. The earliest were probably of Permian age.

Of the remaining animal phyla only the *echinodermata* have contributed large volumes of fossils to build up the sedimentary rock pile. The particular fossils in question are the crinoids mentioned on page 138. In parts of western North America they must have existed by the trillions during Carboniferous times, giving rise to very extensive sheets of crinoidal limestone.

The fossil plants have made a surprisingly large contribution to the sedimentary rocks. Coal we have mentioned, and the very tiny calcareous once-floating algal structures which make up so much chalk. The algae have in fact been immensely important as limestone rock-builders and coral-cementers for much of the Phanerozoic eon. The algal *stromatolites*, referred to above, are rather columnar or cushion-shaped mounds of calcareous material and were perhaps the first of all calcareous organisms. Most reefs today are held together by the growth products of the coralline algae, and reefs in the past seem to have been similarly dependent upon the coral-algal partnership.

Siliceous rocks made very largely of the tiny algae, *diatoms*, are not common but they occur as diatomite in ancient lake deposits. Diatomaceous oozes are also accumulating on parts of the ocean floor. Being so fine-grained and absorbent, diatomite was once used in the manufacture of dynamite.

CHAPTER 10

WHEELS WITHIN WHEELS:
THE GEOLOGICAL CYCLES

OUR book has been concerned with the materials of geology, all of which play their part in the history and evolution of our planet. Minerals tell us something about the orderly way in which elements combine into compounds and how the shapes of crystals are related to the three-dimensional arrangements of atoms. Rocks show us how a number of common minerals may combine in various ways within the outer crust of the earth and how subsequently they may be destroyed or altered. From the sedimentary rocks we read tales of long-vanished land, and sea-scapes, and the orderly rearrangement of mineral matter in bodies of water. Metamorphic rocks bear the signs of heat, pressure and movement in the crust of the earth.

Although they are the mere rags and tatters of life of the past, fossils convey to us something of the remarkable evolution of life and its environment over the last few hundred million years. Countless generations and unbelievable millions of lives are represented in our geological column. Somewhere in the very ancient rocks the traces of how life began may be preserved. Meanwhile the geologist and the biochemist are as busy as bees searching for clues in the rocks and experimenting in the laboratory to answer the question of how life began. It is the same with many questions in geology, and throughout science for that matter. We begin to see how the many different aspects of, or kinds of, science are related to one another. In this book it must be obvious how much the geologist owes to other sciences. Yet there are two ways in which his contribution is unique. He shows how the materials of the world are related to one another and he can demonstrate the long passage of time during which evolution has brought the earth and life to where they are today.

The comparison of the earth with a spaceship is not a bad one. We have on board, so to speak, a fixed quantity of supplies and raw materials, so that when they have been used it may be some time before the system can regenerate them from the waste and rubbish of the past. As in a spaceship, there has to be a source, or sources, of energy. Earth has solar energy to draw upon, its own internal heat, and the force of gravity. Between them these three have kept the geological motors going for several thousand million years.

Yet clearly the world is not the place it was at the beginning of that time. It has changed, used energy from within and from the sun, and has reorganized the materials at least on its surface many times. Its evolution seems to have involved the production of an increasing array of more highly organized things. Where in early Precambrian times there may have been only a few kinds of sedimentary rocks on the surface, now there is a tremendous variety. Precambrian life was simple, with not very many different kinds of organisms – at least compared with the splendid parade of plants and animals we can watch today. There is good reason for believing that when organisms die and decompose the elements within them are released ·from the structures life had built up to be used again in other ways by other organisms. The same atoms must have taken part in the functioning of many different generations, perhaps passing from living into non-

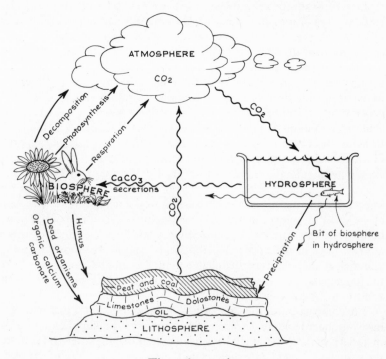

The carbon cycle.

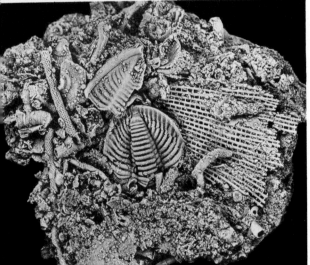

PLATE 23. *Above,* 'Marston Marble', a limestone made very largely of ammonites (Promicroceras). Marston Magna, Somerset. About natural size. *Centre,* trilobite, bryozoan and other fossil debris in the Lower Carboniferous near Bristol. About twice natural size *Below,* a shale from the Coal Measures bearing impressions of several different kinds of plants. About one quarter natural size.

PLATE 24. *Above* a limestone from the Lower Carboniferous of Somerset showing several species of brachiopod. About one quarter natural size. *Centre,* shell bed from the Lower Jurassic of Gloucestershire containing the common fossil curved bivalve *Gryphaea,* columnals of the crinoid *Pentacrinites* and fragments of other organisms. About one quarter natural size. *Below,* a limestone from the Upper Jurassic of Wiltshire in which large bivalves (*Myophorella*) are preserved as casts and moulds. About one eighth natural size.

living matter and back again many times. Some of them, such as the radioactive atoms, are easy to recognize and follow from one place or body to another. Others we can follow simply because they are so common. If we take carbon as an example we may start with carbon dioxide in the atmosphere. It becomes incorporated in a plant by photosynthesis and may rest there as part of a sugar or other organic compound. The plant may be eaten by an animal and the sugar passes into the animal body. There it eventually is used in other chemical actions to provide energy; the by-products of this process may include carbon dioxide. We may say our carbon has completed a cycle. Most of the elements spread across the surface of the planet are involved in cycles of some sort. Many such cycles are small, taking a short time to complete; others involve millions of years.

GEOCHEMICAL CYCLES

In the outermost layers of the earth, which are the only layers directly accessible to us, there are abundant signs of how intimately biological and geological processes have worked together. The way in which carbon is distributed and involved in these processes is perhaps the best illustration of this. The biosphere figures in the geological, or more specifically geochemical, cycle of carbon; and it does so for many of the cycles of many other elements too.

We might picture the general trackways for the cycle of a good number of elements rather as shown below.

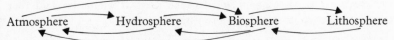

Of course it helps to know something of the chemistry of the 'spheres', but sampling them is a problem. Obviously the lithosphere is too vast to be characterized by a single rock sample. Although we have in the past pages discussed a few of the rocks and minerals in it, there are many others that are important. There is, nevertheless, a broad agreement as to the proportions of the different elements that are present in the crust of the planet.

The hydrosphere seems more uniform. The principal variation within it is that sea water is different from fresh. The atmosphere too is remarkably uniform in composition. Basically it has 78% nitrogen, 21% of oxygen and 1% of a mixture of several other gases.

The biosphere, composed of living things, is made up of carbon, oxygen, hydrogen combined into hydrocarbons, fats, proteins, and so

R.   K

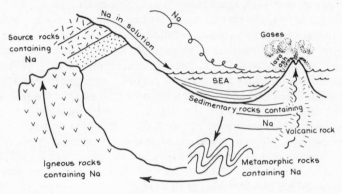

The sodium cycle.

on, with minute traces of many other elements such as nitrogen, phosphorus and sulphur.

In the geochemical cycles the elements may circulate freely between the 'spheres' or be removed and trapped for long periods in one or other 'sphere'. Geological and biological processes tend to select different elements in this way. The process of crystallization in rocks tends to group certain elements together. They may be released or separated when rock is weathered and eroded. Soluble materials are separated from insoluble during erosion, and where water enters the picture life processes can begin to take part. It might be said that water lubricates the cycle in more ways than one.

THE UNIVERSAL SOLVENT

There seems to be a cycle for every element, as there does for many compounds too. At one stage or another along the routes on which our restless atoms move they become involved with a particularly versatile breed of molecule – water. Indeed, many of the cycles would not be possible without it. Minerals, rocks, fossils, all seem to call upon the services of the commonest fluid on earth at some stage in their history. Some scientists have even regarded water as a mineral. It is certainly an essential and natural constituent of the earth, produced without the influence of life. (It can, of course, also be produced by living things.) No other chemical compound seems to have such a

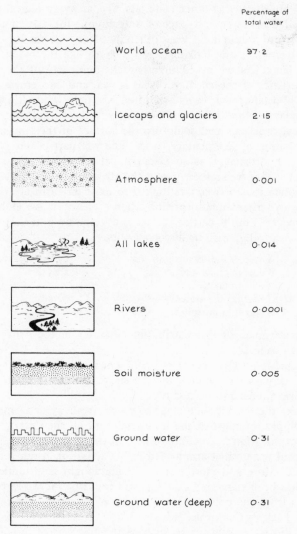

		Percentage of total water
	World ocean	97·2
	Icecaps and glaciers	2·15
	Atmosphere	0·001
	All lakes	0·014
	Rivers	0·0001
	Soil moisture	0·005
	Ground water	0·31
	Ground water (deep)	0·31

The distribution of water. (Data from U.S. Geol. Survey: after Press and Siever).

capacity for dissolving other materials, and many geological processes are speeded up by the presence of water in one form or another.

The world would be a very different place without its water – a desert, devoid of life, looking perhaps more like the moon than our home planet. As we noted in other chapters, one of the foremost characteristics of the earth is that it is wet, and its wetness has been an all-important factor in its evolution. Not only would life as it is on earth today be impossible without water, but so would many of the geological processes that sculpture the surface of the land and cause the deposition of sedimentary rocks. The wet part of our planet, the water or hydrosphere, is so essential yet so widely and intricately distributed that we scarcely give it the attention it deserves.

The quantities of water estimated to exist on earth are enormous, but this is perhaps not surprising when a glance at the globe reveals that some 71% of the earth's surface is covered by water. Most of this cover is sea water, with its dissolved salts.

Water in the oceans and seas	97% of all water
Water in snow and ice	2.25%
Water in lakes	
Underground water	} 0.75%
Water in atmosphere	

Another estimate of the distribution of water in the hydrosphere is shown on page 147.

A surprisingly high figure is that for ice and snow. If the climate were to grow warm enough for the snow and ice to melt, sea level might rise almost 150 m (400 ft).

Despite the overall abundance of water, fresh water seems to be in short supply for most of the industrial, and all the desert, countries in the world. Man has polluted many of the streams, lakes, and even the coastal waters that are needed in his activities, if not for his very existence. More and more water is being sought from underground, and it has been suggested that supplies could be increased by towing icebergs from the polar regions to parts of the world where they are needed, such as California.

How did water come to be such an integral part of the outer layer of our planet? There are several different ideas about the origin of the hydrosphere. Space research has confirmed that earth is the only planet which has a true hydrosphere. Other planets are too hot or too cold to allow water to exist in its liquid state. Elsewhere it is either puffed up into water vapour or it is frozen into ice crystals. It is worth considering how the hydrosphere came into being here on earth.

The Origin of the Hydrosphere

Signs of the presence of water on the earth go back a long way and we believe that it was one of the important original constituents of the planet. When a volcano erupts it releases enormous quantities of water vapour. Some volcanoes seem to have more gas and water vapour within them than others. Experiments in the laboratory show that considerable amounts of water can occur in molten rock and that the amount contained may vary with the temperature and pressure of the melt. Such molten rocks can theoretically contain as much as 10% by weight of water.

When the earth first began to orbit the sun as a planet rather than as a cloud of gas and dust, as some geologists believe, it seems to have

The evolution of the hydrosphere. A, The earth condenses and congeals from hot fluid and gaseous matter. B, Volcanic activity continues to allow gases to escape from the interior giving rise to an atmosphere of hot clouds of water vapour. C, As temperatures continue to drop rains pour down from the clouds, but all is still hot. D, After a long time temperatures have dropped sufficiently for there to be a layer of water over parts of the earth and an atmosphere above. Interaction between the two is ceaseless. (After Fagan).

become very hot. There was no hydrosphere or atmosphere as we know them, but as volcanic activity became an almost universal feature of the surface of the planet the water vapour and gases held within the rock matter were released. A hot envelope of gas accumulated around the planet. As time went by the earth cooled slowly and before long it was cool enough for rain to fall in boiling hot showers and storms. The rain slowly accumulated in the hollows and depressions in the crust, and eventually the ocean basins were filled with water. As the rain ran over the volcanic land surface it began a chain of chemical reactions with the minerals – rock weathering. Sediment was formed and swept away by the streams into the hollows and seas. The geological cycle as we know it had begun, like a large wheel beginning to turn because a smaller cog – the hydrological cycle – had been set in motion.

Since then the waters have cooled and have continued to play an essential part in sculpturing the surface of the earth.

The Hydrological Cycle

Water in the air falls to earth; sometimes it is rain, sometimes snow. Water on the earth tends to run downhill, eventually reaching the sea – or at least some of it does. The rest may be taken up by plants, consumed by animals or just evaporated back into the atmosphere. Constantly it is on the move in the hydrological cycle. The recognition of this fact came slowly. Leonardo da Vinci had a true explanation for

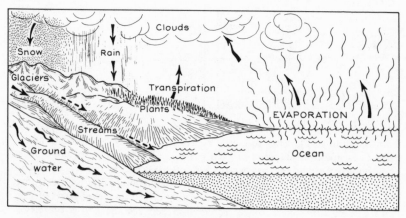

The hydrological cycle.

springs and rivers in the sixteenth century, but it was not until nearly a hundred years later that anyone made the first quantitative investigation of the relation between rainfall and stream flow. Since then geologists have quite discarded the old ideas about great subterranean seas being tapped by springs and being supplied by whirlpools in the oceans.

A diagram explains most quickly the ways in which water may travel between falling to the ground as rain and returning to the atmosphere. We can see at a glance what the pathways are, but to find out how rapidly water may move along them is rather more difficult. There is a continuous exchange of water between the atmosphere and the seas and oceans. An ingenious calculation suggests that the water vapour in the atmosphere amounts to about 25 mm of liquid water per square centimetre of the earth's surface. The average rainfall of the world is nearly 1000 mm per year, so that the average length of time that a molecule of water floats around in the atmosphere – as distinct from being in the sea or elsewhere – is about nine days.

As it moves from one place to another our molecule of water, together of course with millions of others, may play several roles. It may help in the chemical and physical breakdown of mineral matter. It may help wash away the mineral particles and dissolve the soluble minerals. It may be drawn into a plant root or gulped by an animal. Some water remains trapped in sediment as it forms on the sea floor and helps redistribute mineral matter within this sediment to cement it into a cohesive rock.

In volcanoes we see steam from within the earth rising to escape and join the hydrosphere. Perhaps an equal quantity is carried into the crust as water-containing strata are drawn deep below the surface by earth movements.

The ever-growing need for supplies of fresh water drives us to ponder how to make better use of the hydrological cycle. Already man has so polluted the most accessible parts of the cycle that locally the consequences to life have been disastrous. Pollution of rivers by industrial effluents, sewage, insecticides or fertilizers is serious in many parts of the world. The Great Lakes of North America have been terribly damaged by pollution from the cities around them. There are other ways too in which man's use, or misuse, of his environment is having a geological effect via rivers. It was recently calculated that the rivers draining from eastern U.S.A. into the Atlantic are carrying a sediment load four or five times greater than it would be had the area remained uninhabited. What the consequences of this will be in the long run is hard to see, but muddier rivers seem here to stay.

THE ROCK CYCLE

In the course of this book we have looked at minerals and rocks, the basic materials of geology, and at fossils, the traces of life on earth. It was suggested at the beginning that there are definite relationships among igneous, sedimentary and metamorphic rocks. As time passes, and with changing conditions, any one of these rock types may be changed into another form. Earth materials are constantly on the move and we can conveniently show the paths that they follow in our diagram of the rock cycle. The outer circle represents the complete cycle, but there are short-cuts across it that can be taken. To keep the cycle moving there is energy from within the earth and solar energy to help along the processes of weathering, transportation of sedimentary materials, and so on.

This was outlined in our first chapter, and the greater part of this book has been concerned with a look at the materials moving along the pathways of the cycle and with the influence that life has had during part of this movement.

All this may look a nice tidy synthesis – a little over-simplified perhaps – but nevertheless an up-to-date appraisal of how minerals and rocks may fit into a reasonable picture. Yet it was a concept clearly seen by a Scots physician, James Hutton, nearly two hundred years ago. Hutton gave a series of lectures to the Royal Society of Edinburgh in 1785 on the topic and it lead to the publication of a book entitled *Theory of the Earth* (Edinburgh, 1795). Hutton's words have been quoted by many authors and he sums up the rock cycle very successfully in the style of his day: 'We are thus led to see a circulation in the

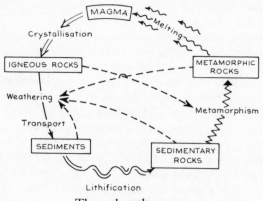

The rock cycle.

manner of this globe, and a system of beautiful economy in the works of nature. This earth, like the body of an animal, is wasted in the same time that it is repaired. It has a state of growth and augmentation; it has another state, which is diminution and decay. This world is thus destroyed in one part, but it is renewed in another; and the operations by which this world is thus constantly renewed are as evident to the scientific eye as are those in which it is necessarily destroyed.'

Hutton would be pleased to know how his theory has been accepted over the years. Today's geologist uses equipment far more complex than Hutton may have dreamed of, and in a lifetime he may see more geology than a dozen men could in Hutton's day. But he has to use the same discipline that Hutton applied: careful observation, accurate note making – or data gathering as it may be called today – and a reasoned attempt to account for what has been discovered in the light of what was known before. With so many scientists at work in the twentieth century a piece of 'science' may be out of date almost before the printer's ink is dry on the page. If science needed anything to make it even more exciting, perhaps the speed with which it is being produced today adds that touch.

The Rocks Display'd – a version of the rock cycle by Dr Gilbert Wilson. (By permission of the Council of the Geologists' Association).

BOOKS TO READ

THERE is a growing 'footage' of good little geology books to be found on library shelves. The following are some of those that seem to be specially attractive, and which are relatively simple and inexpensive. Larger, expensive books abound, and there are many paperbacks at a more advanced level.

General Reading

AGER, D. V. *Introducing Geology*. Faber, London, 2nd edition, 1975.
ROBSON, D. *The Science of Geology*. Blandford Press, London, 1972. *The Story of the Earth*. Geological Museum, H.M.S.O., 1972.

Rocks and Minerals

KIRKALDY, J. F. *Minerals and Rocks in Colour*. Blandford Press, London, 1963.
PEARL, R. M. *How to know Minerals and Rocks*. McGraw, 1965.
POUGH, F. H. *A Field Guide to Rocks and Minerals*. Constable, London, 1970.
ROGERS, C. *Rocks and Minerals*. Ward Lock, London, 1973.
SORRELL C. A., *The Rocks and Minerals of the World*, Collins, London, 1976.
WATSON, J. *Rocks and Minerals*. George Allen and Unwin, London, 1973.

Fossils

BARRETT, J. *Life on the Sea Shore*. Collins: Countryside Series, London, 1974.
BROUWER, A. *General Palaeontology*. Oliver and Boyd, London and Edinburgh, 1967.
CLARK, D. L. *Fossils, Paleontology and Evolution*. Wm. C. Brown Co., Publishers, Iowa. 1968.
COX, B. *Prehistoric Animals*. Hamlyn all-colour paperbacks, London, 1969.
KIRKALDY, J. F. *The Study of Fossils*. Hutchinson Educational, London, 1963. *Fossils in colour*. Blandford Press, London, 1967.
MCALESTER, A. L. *The History of Life*. Foundations of Earth Science Series, Prentice-Hall Inc., New Jersey, 1968.
MIDDLEMISS, F. A. *Fossils*. George Allen and Unwin Ltd., London, 1969.
RHODES, F. H. T., ZIM, H. S. and SHAFFER, P. R. *Fossils: a guide to prehistoric life*. Paul Hamlyn Ltd., London. 1965.

INDEX

Figures in **bold** type refer to plate numbers